WHERE
GOD
HAPPENS

A World Community of
Christian Meditation Book

WHERE GOD HAPPENS

DISCOVERING CHRIST IN ONE ANOTHER

Rowan Williams

Foreword by Desmond Tutu

Introduction by Laurence Freeman

NEW SEEDS
Boston
2005

NEW SEEDS BOOKS
An imprint of
Shambhala Publications, Inc.
Horticultural Hall
300 Massachusetts Avenue
Boston, Massachusetts 02115
www.shambhala.com

9 8 7 6 5 4 3 2 1

First Edition
Printed in the United States of America

♾ This edition is printed on acid-free paper that meets the
American National Standards Institute z39.48 Standard.
Distributed in the United States by Random House, Inc.,
and in Canada by Random House of Canada Ltd

Library of Congress Cataloging-in-Publication Data
Williams, Rowan, 1950–
Where God happens: discovering Christ in one another/
Rowan Williams; foreword by Desmond Tutu; introduction
by Laurence Freeman.—1st ed.
p. cm.
Includes bibliographical references (p.   ).
ISBN 1-59030-231-1 (hardcover: alk. paper)
1. Spiritual life—Christianity. 2. Spirituality. 3. Desert Fathers. I. Title.
BV4501.3.W553 2005
248.4—dc22
2005007754

CONTENTS

FOREWORD

I have not ceased to be amazed by the audiences I have had the good fortune to address in the United States. One would have expected them to pooh-pooh some of the notions I have alluded to in my speeches. One has been told about the rampant materialism and consumerism of that great land, of the relentless pursuit of individual success that has spawned a cynical attitude in many of them. But when I have spoken about transcendence and goodness, about gentleness and compassion, about generosity and sharing, instead of being rebuffed or having people storm out in exasperation, I have been very pleasantly surprised at how eagerly these audiences have lapped it all up.

But in fact I should not have been surprised, because that hunger for the spiritual is ultimately integral to what it means to be human. Did not Saint Augustine of Hippo sum it up well when he declared, "[God,] Thou hast made us for thyself and our hearts are restless until they find their rest in thee"? Extraordinarily, we are almost the ultimate paradox, the finite made for the infinite, in that we all have an ontological hunger for God and only God can satisfy that hunger.

So my American audiences were really doing that which comes naturally, as the old song puts it. Yes, in the midst of the confusion and anxiety and fear, in the time of rabid competitiveness to see who will own the most, the largest, there is a deep, deep hunger for spiritual things; yes, for God, and we have often let people desperately down through we in the Church offering them less than the best, offering them less than what they really need: God.

How interesting, indeed almost contradictory, that in cultures that are so aggressive, so hard-nosed and cynical, so grasping, so ferociously competitive, so obsessed with success, those we most admire are people such as Mother Teresa, who could be described in many ways, though "macho" would not be one of them; the Dalai Lama; Nelson Mandela; and so on. We revere them ultimately because they are good, and our internal antennae hone in on them because we are those made for goodness, for love, for compassion, for God, and, yes, our hearts will remain forever restless until we find our true rest only in God.

And so we want to be helped, all of us, not just Americans, to find our way back home to our true rest. We need those who are wise in the ways of the spirit who will instruct us all how to be in touch with the source of all being, who will teach us how to become truly human by teaching us the things of the spirit.

Some of the best such teachers were the Egyptian mothers and fathers who left the cities to found the desert communities, the forerunners of our religious communities today. Their encounters with God and the things of God taught them many truths, especially about how to grow in holiness, being patient with oneself, eschewing harsh judgment of others while being hard on oneself, dying to the neighbor in order for both to live for God, fleeing status and dignity and chatter to be still in contemplation of God whose love has removed our sin. We are those called to stillness, avoiding the bane of our day, our frenetic busyness that ineffectually tries to hide our deep anxiety and insecurity and fearfulness. We are too scared to experience the stillness that will let us know our intrinsic worth, a free gift of God's grace, and we obtrude ourselves between God and our neighbor when we could know the blessedness of putting our neighbor in touch with God, when God can then happen, and we then can know the double blessing that blesses both the giver and the receiver, and no one knows which they are and it does not matter.

How blessed that we should be given a splendid introduction to and brief commentary on those mothers and fathers by perhaps the best theologian in the Anglican Communion, undoubtedly the best living communicator

of the Gospel verities, in the person of the present Archbishop of Canterbury, Rowan Williams. Yes, God's world
needs, as he points out so convincingly, a Church renewed in contemplation. It is good to know that the
desert mothers and fathers said we all can be contemplatives and that we can have our deserts in the crowded
places where we live and work. We thank God for this
splendid volume and for The World Community for
Christian Meditation.

I must take to heart one of the admonitions from the
desert saints, having been mentioned somewhat favorably
in the book: I should flee to my cell to weep over my sins.

DESMOND M. TUTU
Archbishop Emeritus

PREFACE

This little book is meant as a modest contribution to the discovery of a church renewed in contemplation, across the cultural frontiers of our world.

It began its journey to its present form through the invitation to lead the John Main Seminar for 2001 in Sydney, Australia. This came as a great surprise and delight, and I want to express the warmest of thanks to The World Community for Christian Meditation for this opportunity. Father Laurence Freeman helped and supported me in any number of ways before and during this event, for which I am very grateful, and I owe him a still greater debt of gratitude for his cooperation in editing the talks and discussions of the seminar into their present form.

To speak of the desert tradition in Australia had and has a special resonance: Australia is a country with the desert at its heart, a desert that it has only begun to explore spiritually. The strong sense at the 2001 seminar of an impulse in the Australian churches to engage more seriously with this was profoundly moving for all those present from other countries. And of course, to speak of the desert tradition at an event commemorating John Main had its own appropriateness, given that Father John was one of those who most effectively put the tradition to work in our own day. The roots of his distinctive spirituality lie deep in the fourth and fifth centuries, especially in the work of that great expositor of the desert world, John Cassian. The World Community, which continues his mission, is for me, as for many throughout the world, a taste of what a committedly contemplative church might look and feel like, with its intense fidelity to shared silence as well as shared belief and experience.

At root it all has to do with whether we believe that religion is about fullness of life or about control. For example, religious education, when it is doing its job of "educating the spirit," has to be the conveying—in all aspects of the educational environment—of what I call the peaceful worthwhileness of each person. The person as he or she is at rest is worthwhile, just as they are. From that God will move. God will create. God will change. My fascination with religious education in the primary school focuses on the messages that are given by the educational institution to the child about that peaceful worthwhileness. It is a wonderful sight to see several hundred children sitting in silence in a meeting hall. Their silence has not been forced upon them; they are simply being allowed to sit and be quiet. I believe that this opportunity for silence is much more important to religious formation than simply being taught about religion.

As time passes it will be harder to think that the church in the future will take one clear and uniform institutional shape across the globe or even throughout local communities. In some areas, the church is already beginning to exist in parallel lines, not in sealed compartments, but in different styles and idioms and with real interchange. This actually puts more rather than less of a burden on those called to leadership or pastoral oversight. They have the job of orchestrating these differences into something other than competition and disharmony. I find that a significant part of my daily work as a bishop.

I strongly believe that the promise that the church will not fail can be relied on. This is because the church is the community of those whom Jesus calls to receive the Spirit and to share the relation that he has to his Father, his source. Jesus does not stop issuing that invitation, and so the church does not stop existing. That, to me, is the bottom line.

My first serious acquaintance with the monastic literature of the desert came by way of friendship with one of the greatest contemporary scholars and expositors of the tradition, Sister Benedicta Ward, at the time when she was first engaged in translating the material for her classic version of the most significant text, *The Sayings of the Desert*

Fathers. Like everyone else who has worked in this area, I owe her a lasting and incalculable debt.

Almost every time I have tried to write a book, I have discovered in the last stages of composition that someone else is about to publish a better one on more or less the same subject, which is a pity for me but very helpful for everyone else. This time the book in question was John Chryssavgis's study *In the Heart of the Desert: The Spirituality of the Desert Fathers and Mothers*. I am delighted to be able to include a couple of quotations from what will undoubtedly be a work of lasting value.

My final work on the text was done during a stay at the Monastery of Bose in northern Italy. The welcome of the community was quite unforgettable, and it is a pleasure to dedicate this book to a group of men and women who are such a sign of the continuing vitality of the contemplative life in a thoroughly contemporary mode.

ROWAN WILLIAMS

A NOTE ON THE SOURCES

The sayings and stories associated with the first generations of Christian monks and nuns in the Egyptian desert
were evidently being collected orally during or soon after
their lifetimes. But the development of written collections took longer, and the written material we have inevitably shows signs of editing, signs of concern about
issues that may not have been that important in the "real
time" of the stories, and so on. The generations most lib-
erally represented in the oldest sayings collections are
those who flourished between about 350 and about
450—though the most influential figure, Anthony the
Great, was most active just before this period and died at
the age of 105 in 356.

Many of the figures remembered in the tradition
therefore lived through years of acute crisis in the Egyptian monastic world. Around 400, the Egyptian communities—and their friends and supporters elsewhere—were
bitterly divided over theological matters. The detail is
hard to pin down objectively at times, since most reports

are heavily slanted, but it was broadly about the influence
of speculative and philosophical ideas on theology—especially those ideas associated with the great third-century
Alexandrian teacher Origen, brilliant but theologically
suspect. In particular, there was concern as to whether his
teaching, or teachings derived from it, encouraged a false
attitude toward the human body (and thus to the incar-
nation of God in Jesus Christ). Traces of this conflict
can be found here and there in the literature. Archbishop
Theophilus, a fierce opponent of the Origenist party, is
sometimes presented in a rather ambivalent light. He was
responsible for the exile of several leading ascetics from
Egypt, and those who later settled in Palestine were certainly among those who helped to give shape to the tradition of the sayings as we have them. But equally there is
a certain lukewarmness in the presentation of a figure
such as Evagrius, the foremost theologian of the Origenist
group and an immense influence on many later figures. It
is as if the literature were trying to pick its way through
explosive territory. Stories about dramatic physical manifestations of God's grace in prayer—the flames shooting
from the raised hands of a monk praising God in solitude—may reflect a concern to steer away from too much
suspicion of the material world. But again, stories center-
ing on the hard work of daily and unrewarding labor may
register a caution against looking for too much visible
drama. And the various ways in which "thoughts" are dis-

cussed—it is really a technical term for distracting or even obsessive mental activity—often indicates a familiarity with the vocabulary of Evagrius's circle.

One could go on spotting these telltale signs of a context more complicated than the surface suggests, but the point is that by the time the major early collections had been assembled in something like their present form—in the first half of the fifth century probably—they were being used as fundamentally coherent guides to the life of prayer and asceticism. There are obvious differences of emphasis, and sometimes more than that, but these were evidently seen as part of a discipline that did not seek to produce lifeless uniformity. As the following pages will, I hope, make clear, there is a healthy readiness to live with the variety of perspectives and to respect the living diversity of monastic discipline. It is this that makes the sayings traditions so endlessly intriguing and stretching—and it is this that has meant their survival and constant "recycling" across the centuries.

The two great early collections in Greek, the "Alphabetical" and the "Anonymous," are the source for practically everything discussed here: the former tells stories associated with specific people from the first monastic generations; the latter groups sayings and stories by subject (and suggests, incidentally, what other evidence confirms: that there were several stories that could attach themselves to different names or no name at all). Both collections have been translated in their entirety by Sister Benedicta Ward in a most accessible form. My translations in this book owe a great deal to her, as will be clear, but I have not always followed the same choice of idiom.

Introduction

The growth and expansion of Christian monasticism in the deserts of Egypt from the mid-third century is an extraordinary phenomenon. I use the present tense here because, as Rowan Williams illustrates in his exposition of the wisdom of this movement, it is a phenomenon that is still with us. We may not be able to understand it fully, but if its power to fascinate captures even those who do not share the faith of the desert fathers and mothers, then even the attempt to understand it will enrich and stimulate our global spiritual awareness. It is a very contemporary spirituality.

These monastic oddballs of an unimaginably different and ancient world may indeed hold a secret for our modern world that no economist, sociologist, politician, or religious leader can match. The desert wisdom teaches rather than preaches. Its authority is experiential, not theoretical. The upshot of this is a phenomenon that many modern people, disenchanted with religious institutionalism, will find unusual—a religious group that is grasped by the absolute experience of God and is uncompromising in its desire to be one with that experience while remaining humorous, humble and, above all, not condemning of those of other beliefs or practice.

As Rowan Williams elegantly describes, the teachers of the desert were striking *individuals*. They loved and sought solitude. But they were also *persons* held in a network of realistic relationships in community. When they began to leave the towns and villages of the fertile inhabited regions of the Nile Delta and settle, at first, in the inhospitable "exterior desert," it was partly because of the persecution of Christians by Decius. But even after the persecution subsided, the monks remained. Furthermore, they began to plunge deeper into the "full desert," as they called it. They renounced the socioeconomic world and family life as completely as Indian sannyasis. However, their collected sayings—the substance of the teaching that has descended to us—show it was not a misanthropy or hatred of the world. It was renunciation, *not* rejection; a passion for the absolute but not intolerance or fundamentalism; and above all, not self-righteousness.

They knew how easy it is for religious people to fall into the self-contradictory sin of pride, and the monks of the desert feared this pitfall more than any other. This was why they kept seeking deeper desert, to escape the fame that began early on to attach itself to them. They were not very well-adjusted individuals if we look at them from the standards of the worldly success they had abandoned. Yet if we judge them by what they believed, they had an authenticity and simplicity about them that still touches our hearts and wins our admiration.

They were fighters, not escapees, pilgrims, not tourists. That this phenomenon erupted where it did is perhaps because religion and geography are not unaligned. In no other country does the desert come so close to the populated world. It is not an abstract idea, as the "bush" or the "wilderness" can be to modern people. The desert is always present to the Egyptian in the dramatic contrast between the rich black soil of the Nile Valley and the sterile sand of the desert. Herodotus was the first to remark on the intensely religious nature of the Egyptian people, for whom religious truth was both the commonest and the highest of all values. This geography and religious passion had earlier been the ancient setting of the conflict between Osiris and Horus, the Egyptian gods of life, and Seth, the god of opposition and negation. The desert fathers and mothers were fighting the ancient fight—whose main scene of operation is the human heart—but with the new weapon of their faith in the power and reality of Christ.

Following their legendary pioneer Saint Anthony, they plunged farther and farther into the desert and formed the eremitical centers of Nitria, the Cells, and Scetis. By the end of the fourth century, the old men were grumbling about there being too many monks, five thousand in Nitria alone, it was estimated, and six hundred in the even remoter Cells. Pilgrims, seekers, and tourists came, some just to bug them, others to sit seriously at their feet and continue the lineage. One of these visitors, who stayed twenty years, was a young man from present-day Romania called John Cassian. Early in the fifth century he returned to Europe and established a monastic community for men and women in Marseilles. The ideal of desert monasticism had already reached as far as the west coast of Ireland. But it was an influence largely dependent on the already famous collections of the "sound bites" of the fathers' sayings, with their striking similarity at times to Zen stories, and what there was of direct personal experience. Cassian agreed to a request by a local bishop, anxious about the unruliness of the monastic movement—still an untamed lay movement—to compose a more methodical presentation of the teachings of the desert wisdom. His great work the *Conferences of the Fathers* was the result. A generation later Saint Benedict, who had himself begun his monastic life on the desert model, recommended in his Rule that the *Conferences* should be read every day at mealtimes. By these stages and connections the spiritual pioneers of the Egyptian desert entered deeply into the mind and culture of Western society.

The monasticism they thus inspired and that Benedict organized and adapted to Western conditions became a major shaping force in European civilization. Through the Dark Ages, which followed the collapse of Rome as the sole superpower, the Rule of Benedict inspired and sustained an alternative form of life. It was a life in hardworking, economically self-sufficient communities conscious of their responsibilities to the world around them but practicing a gospel form of the radical detachment exemplified by the desert fathers. The Benedictine life, about which Rowan Williams has also taught, was itself a civilizing force because it worked through the contagious power of example rather than by the force of imposing uniformity. What was so attractive and influential about the Benedictine lifestyle? Surely its understanding of the human need for peace in any lifestyle that promises sustainable growth in personal development. Holiness—or wholeness as people prefer to say today—requires a degree of inner and outer peace that respects the at times conflicting, though not contradictory, demands of body, mind, and spirit. The first requirement for this peace or harmony is order in human living and a right use of time. This is what Benedict so brilliantly and calmly concentrates on—a community that respects differences but controls the ego while managing time realistically around the central priority of prayer.

Maybe the Rule "saved civilization," but it is still, according to Benedict himself, just a beginning in the spiritual journey. For him the ideal of the desert father was never far from sight. Externally this might mean that after years in the monastery the monk would move into a form of solitude. Interiorly it should mean that prayer becomes increasingly "pure." That means that it is more centered in and characterized by the silence of the heart and less in the images and concepts of mental prayer or in external ritual. Western monasticism institutionally forgot this. Inevitably, then, the institution ossified and its considerable political and economic influence collapsed. Not one English monastic community resisted its dissolution and appropriation by the state in the sixteenth century. Today the monastic movement continues, although often without quite knowing why, or how it should relate to the wider world. The heady days of the Egyptian desert are still studied but seem very archaic to most monks. Many monasteries have closed or are contracting for lack of vocations. Yet the greater wonder is that they are still there, testifying, sometimes to their own amazement, to the inextinguishable flame of the monastic archetype in the human psyche that Benedict summarized as "seeking God."

In 1969 John Main, an Irish Benedictine, was going through a difficult chapter of his own life. There was conflict in his community in London and he had been sent to a monastery in the United States. He became headmaster of its school and struggled with the cultural revolution underway but also learned from it. When a young student, like a modern-day Cassian, visited and asked John Main for an introduction to Christian mysticism, the *Conferences of the Fathers* proved its mysterious and enduring power of inspiration. This led John Main to read Cassian again, no longer to pass exams but to answer questions about contemporary spiritual hunger. In the Tenth Conference, "On Prayer," he came across the radiant nucleus of desert spirituality, a forgotten key to the prayer of the heart. In this conference Cassian addresses the practice of prayer and its practical difficulties, the greatest of which, and root of them all, is distraction. The remedy he advises is the simple practice of meditation in the faith-filled repetition of a single formula, or mantra. Main realized this was a pearl of spiritual teaching. More than a *lectio*, or reading of Scripture, more than a cultivation of inner quietness, he saw it was a spiritual discipline, an ascesis of the kind necessary to effect serious and sustainable change in the person praying. His own experience of learning meditation in Asia before he became a monk had helped him to recognize the specific value and meaning of Cassian's recommendation and then to pick up the thread of this teaching throughout the Christian tradition.

Thus the seed of The World Community for Christian Meditation was planted. Or rather, thus it fell from the fertile seedbed of desert wisdom. Just as an ancient desert father attracted disciples just by sitting in meditation, so around the teaching of John Main a community was formed. The pattern is ever the same—it is this sameness that makes the desert wisdom so very fresh and useful to us. But the form it takes today is different. A more than local phenomenon has resulted. There are no more Nitrias and Scetises on the same scale. But through the practice of Christian meditation, the desert wisdom has led to a global community reflecting the "new holiness" of the modern world. The new monks of the Christian world have a new look. Some live in traditional monasteries, but the majority do not. Many are integrating what previously seemed impossible to reconcile—deep spiritual practice and conjugal love, solitude and social responsibility.

Contemporary holiness needs to acknowledge the expansion of the human mind into a multicultural and indeed multifaith communion. And this is the enormous challenge to Christianity today. Either it grows into the future with the courage and faith showed by the ancient monks as they penetrated farther and farther into the heart of the desert to find the true God, renouncing the god of their imagining, or—what is the alternative? Only to bury its head in the sand. Deeper faith or ever more superficial fundamentalism is the constant choice of religion—as basic as the struggle between Osiris and Seth or that of the desert fathers with their own fears and desires. As Rowan Williams shows, it is also our personal choice and struggle every day.

What led Rowan Williams into friendship with The World Community for Christian Meditation and to his support for it also led to his giving the 2001 John Main Seminar in Sydney, Australia. The seminar then led to this book, which is an important contribution to the renewal and expansion of the Christian mind today. It reflects his own prophetic perception that one thing always leads to another and that if we trace this sequence back to its origins, we have found the direction we should be moving in.

LAURENCE FREEMAN, OSB
Director, The World Community for Christian Meditation

I.

Life, Death, and Neighbors

I.

One thing that comes out very clearly from any reading of the great desert monastic writers of the fourth and fifth centuries is the impossibility of thinking about contemplation or meditation or "spiritual life" in abstraction from the actual business of living in the body of Christ, living in concrete community. The life of intimacy with God in contemplation is both the fruit and the course of a renewed style of living together. These reflections on the legacy of the fathers and mothers of the desert consider how they saw the whole of this life together, where they thought contemplation came from and where it led to. They point to the wellsprings of renewal in our community as Christians seeking God in prayer and common life. We are always faced with the danger of trying to think about this odd thing called spiritual life as if it were a matter we could deal with in isolation, and it is often very attractive to attempt this, simply because the facts of human life together are normally so messy, so unpromising and unedifying. Other people in their actual material reality do make things a lot more difficult when what we *think* we want is spirituality, the cultivation of a sensitive and rewarding relationship with eternal truth and love. And this is where the desert monastics have an uncompromising message for us: relation with eternal truth and love simply doesn't happen without mending our relations with Tom, Dick, and Harriet. The actual substance of our relation with eternal truth and love is bound up with how we manage the proximity of these human neighbors.

At first sight, this monastic movement seems to have been all about avoiding the compromises that the presence of other human beings entailed. We encounter the very common language of "fleeing" from other people in the writings of the desert, and the impulse of monasticism had a lot to do with the worry felt by increasing numbers of Christians that the church of their day was becoming corrupt and secularized. The early monks and nuns moved off into the communities of the desert because they weren't convinced that the church in its "ordinary" manifestations showed with any clarity what the church was supposed to be about; they wanted to find out what the church really was—which is another way of saying that they wanted to find out what humanity really was when it was in touch with God through Jesus Christ. In the literature associated with the early generations of desert ascetics, they report back from the "laboratory of the Spirit" not only about how prayer is to be experienced but also about how humanity is to be understood—about life, death, and neighbors.

The phrase derives from a saying of Anthony the Great, the earliest and most influential of the Christian desert monastic teachers:

> Our life and our death is with our neighbor. If
> we win our brother, we win God. If we cause
> our brother to stumble, we have sinned against
> Christ.[1]

We can compare this with some material from a generation later that comes to us under the name of Moses the Black (whom we will meet again), one of the most vivid personalities of the early monastic world, a rather larger-than-life character whose teaching and sometimes slightly anarchic example appear in many stories. He was a converted Ethiopian highwayman (large physically and generally larger than life) whose burial place is still shown to visitors near the monastery of Baramous in the desert west of Cairo—one small sign of the extraordinary continuity to be experienced at such sites. Moses is credited with a series of summary proverb-like sayings about the monastic life written for another great teacher, Abba Poemen, one of which seems to pick up the language of Anthony yet give it a twist that is at first sight very puzzling. "The monk," says Moses, "must die to his neighbor and never judge him at all in any way whatever."[2] If our life and our death are with the neighbor, this spells out something of what our "death" with the neighbor might mean: it is to renounce the power of judgment over someone else—a task hard enough indeed to merit being described as death. And the basis of this is elaborated in another of the Moses sayings: in reply to a brother who wants to now what it means to "think in your heart that you are a sinner," which is defined as another of the essentials of the monastic life, Moses says, "If you are occupied with your own faults, you have no time to see those of your neighbor."[3]

We begin to see here the cluster of ideas generated by the apparently simple words of Anthony. Living Christianly with the neighbor, living in such a way that the neighbor is "won"—converted, brought into saving relation with Jesus Christ—involves my "death." I must die to myself, a self understood as the solid possessor of virtues and gifts, entitled to pronounce on the neighbor's spiritual condition. My own awareness of my failure and weakness is indispensable to my communicating the gospel to my neighbor. I put the neighbor in touch with God by a particular kind of detachment from him or her. And, the desert writers insist, this is absolutely basic for our growth in the life of grace. Here is a saying under the name of John the Dwarf:

"You don't build a house by starting with the roof and working down. You start with the foundation."

They said, "What does that mean?"

He said, "The foundation is our neighbor whom we must win. The neighbor is where we start. Every commandment of Christ depends on this."[4]

Everything begins with this vision and hope: to put the neighbor in touch with God in Christ. On this the rest of our Christian life depends, and it entails facing the death of a particular kind of picture of myself. If I fail to put someone in touch with God, I face another sort of death, the death of my relation with Christ, because failing to "win" the neighbor is to stand in the way of Christ, to block Christ's urgent will to communicate with all.

The desert monastics are keenly interested in diagnosing what sort of things get in the way and block someone else's relation with Christ. They seem very well aware that one of the great temptations of religious living is the urge to intrude between God and other people. We love to think that we know more of God than others; we find it comfortable and comforting to try to control the access of others to God. Jesus himself speaks bluntly about this when he describes the religious enthusiasts of his day shutting the door of the Kingdom in the face of others:

"You do not enter yourselves, and when others try to enter, you stop them" (Matt. 23:13). And he goes on to describe how such people exert themselves to gain even one convert, but because they are only trying to make others in their own image, they make them twice as worthy of condemnation as themselves (15). The desert teachers are well aware that by fleeing to the isolation of prayerful communities, they do not automatically leave behind this deep-rooted longing to manage the access of other people to God, and this is why they insist upon an ever-greater honesty about the self; this is why the "manifesting of thoughts" to a senior brother or sister becomes so crucial—because we are all drawn almost irresistibly back toward this urge to manage.

One of the most frequent ways in which this becomes visible, they suggest, is *inattention*, the failure to see what is truly there in front of you—because your own vision is clouded by self-obsession or self-satisfaction. There are several variants of a story in which some young monk goes in despair to one of the great "old men" to say that he has consulted an elder about his temptations and been told to do severe and intolerable penance, and the old man tells the younger one to return to his first counselor and tell him that he has not paid proper attention to the need of the novice. If I don't really know how to attend to the reality that is my own inner turmoil, I shall fail in responding to the needs of someone else. And the desert literature consistently suggests that excessive harshness, a readiness to judge and prescribe, normally has its roots in that kind of inattention to oneself. Abba Joseph responds to the invitation to join in condemning someone by saying, "Who am I?" And the phrase might suggest not just "Who am I to be judging?" but also "How can I pass judgment when I don't know the full truth about myself?"[5]

Among the longest collections of sayings attributed to particular desert fathers are those around the names of Macarius the Great and Poemen (granted that Poemen, "the shepherd," may be a name concealing several different figures), and these collections have in common an exceptional number of sayings on the subject of the dangers of harshness and self-satisfaction. Of Macarius, we read, in an unforgettable image, that "he became like a God on earth" because when he saw the sins of the brothers, he would "cover" them, just as God casts his protection over the world.[6] Informed of a self-confident old monk whose counsel has depressed others, Macarius pays a visit:

> When he was alone with him, the old man
> [Macarius] asked, "How are things going with
> you?" Theopemptus replied, "Thanks to your
> prayers, all is well." The old man asked, "Do
> you not have to battle with your fantasies?"
> He answered, "No, up to now all is well." He
> was afraid to admit anything. But the old man

said to him, "I have lived for many years as an ascetic and everyone sings my praises, but, despite my age, I still have trouble with sexual fantasies." Theopemptus said, "Well, it is the same with me, to tell the truth." And the old man went on admitting, one by one, all the other fantasies that caused him to struggle, until he had brought Theopemptus to admit all of them himself. Then he said, "What do you do about fasting?" "Nothing till the ninth hour," he replied. "Fast till evening and take some exercise," said Macarius. "Go over the words of the gospel and the rest of Scripture. And if an alien thought arises within you, don't look down but up: the Lord will come to your help."[7]

Self-satisfaction is dealt with not by confrontation or condemnation but by the quiet personal exposure of failure in such a way as to prompt the same truthfulness in someone else: the neighbor is won, converted, by Macarius's death to any hint of superiority in his vision of himself. He has nothing to defend, and he preaches the gospel by simple identification with the condition of another, a condition others cannot themselves face honestly. How easy to go in and say, "I *know* you suffer these temptations"; Macarius refuses this easy way and goes instead by the way of "death to the neighbor," refusing to judge and exposing himself to judgment.

But we can find something like the opposite extreme in the stories as well. What about those who judge themselves too harshly? Abba Poemen is confronted with a brother who admits to having committed a great sin and wants to do three years' penance.

> The old man said, "That's a lot." The brother said, "What about one year?" The old man said, "That's still quite a lot." Some other people suggested forty days; Poemen said, "That's a lot too." And he said, "What I think is that if someone repents with all one's heart and intends never to commit the sin again, perhaps God will be satisfied with only three days."[8]

The point of leading someone to confront his or her weakness and need is not to enforce discipline or cement patterns of spiritual superiority and inferiority. Whether it is a matter of persuading others to admit what they have never admitted or of helping them to face mercifully what they *have* admitted, the goal is reconciliation with God by way of this combination of truth and mercy. A harsh judgment of others can lead to despair; several stories turn on this,[9] as we have already seen, when monks resort in fear or self-loathing to one of the great old men after receiving rough treatment from a less-experienced elder. The fundamental need as far as the counselor is concerned is first of all to put oneself on the level of the one who has sinned, to heal by solidarity, not condemnation. Hence stories like that of Moses:

> There was a brother at Scetis who had committed a fault. So they called a meeting and invited Abba Moses. He refused to go. The priest sent someone to say to him, "They're all waiting for you." So Moses got up and set off; he took a leaky jug and filled it with water and took it with him. The others came out to meet him and said, "What is this, father?" The old man said to them, "My sins run out behind me and I cannot see them, yet here I am coming to sit in judgment on the mistakes of somebody else." When they heard this, they called off the meeting.[10]

An anonymous version of the story portrays one of the old men at the same kind of meeting getting up and leaving when sentence is passed. "Where are you going, father?" they ask. "I have just been condemned," he replies.[11] (How wonderfully recognizable is his response—someone had committed a fault, so they called a meeting.) And Abba Bessarion's version:

> A brother who had sinned was turned out of
> the church by the priest. Abba Bessarion got
> up and followed him out; he said, "I too am a
> sinner."[12]

Macarius was like a god in Scetis: he hid what he saw
as if he had not seen it, says the narrative.[13] And,

> A brother questioned Abba Poemen, saying,
> "If I see my brother sinning, should I hide
> the fact?" The old man said, "At the moment
> when we hide a brother's fault, God hides
> our own. At the moment when we reveal a
> brother's fault, God reveals our own."[14]

Poemen again:

> Some old men came to see Abba Poemen
> and said to him, "We see some of the brothers
> falling asleep during divine worship. Should
> we wake them up?" He said, "As for me, when
> I see a brother who is falling asleep during
> the Office, I lay his head on my knees and let
> him rest."[15]

We can be deceived into thinking that the desert
monks and nuns—at least those quoted here—were

somehow indifferent to sin, or that their notion of relation to one another was a matter of bland acceptance. But they are not exponents of some sort of "I'm OK, you're OK" method. They actually believe that sin is immensely serious and that separation from God is a real possibility: if you define the purpose of your life, a costly, boring, difficult life in physically harsh conditions, as "winning your neighbor," you may reasonably be expected to believe that it is a tough and serious business, in which success isn't guaranteed. But they also take for granted that the only way in which you know the seriousness of separation from God is in your own experience of yourself. Moses writes to Poemen, "If you have sin enough in your own life and your own home, you have no need to go searching for it elsewhere." And, more graphically, from Moses again, "If you have a corpse laid out in your own front room, you won't have leisure to go to a neighbor's funeral."[16] This is not about minimizing sin; it is about learning how to recognize it from seeing the cost in yourself. If it can't be addressed by you in terms of your own needs, it can't be addressed anywhere—however seductive it is to say, "I know how to deal with this problem in *your* life— and never mind about mine."

The inattention and harshness that shows we have not grasped this is for so many of the desert fathers and mothers the major way in which we fail in winning the neighbor. Poemen goes so far as to say that it is the one thing about which we can justly get angry with each other.

> A brother asked Abba Poemen, "What does it mean to be angry with your brother without a cause? [The reference is obviously to Matt. 5:21*ff.*] He said, "If your brother hurts you by his arrogance and you are angry with him because of this, that is getting angry without a cause. If he pulls out your right eye and cuts off your right hand and you get angry with him, that is getting angry without a cause. But if he cuts you off from God—then you have every right to be angry with him.[17]

To assume the right to judge, or to assume that you have arrived at a settled spiritual maturity that entitles you to prescribe confidently at a distance for another's sickness, is in fact to leave others without the therapy they need for their souls; it is to cut them off from God, to leave them in their spiritual slavery—while reinforcing your own slavery. Neither you nor they have access to life—as in the words of Jesus, you have shut up heaven for others and for yourself. But the plain acknowledgment of your solidarity in need and failure opens a door: it shows that it is possible to live in the truth and to go forward in hope. It is in such a moment that God gives himself through you, and you become by God's gift a means of connecting another with God. You have done the job you were created to do.

Saint Anthony of the Desert says that gaining the brother or sister and winning God are linked. It is not getting them signed up to something or getting them on your side. It is opening doors for them to healing and to wholeness. Insofar as you open such doors for another, you gain God, in the sense that you become a place where God happens for somebody else. *You become a place where God happens.* God comes to life for somebody else in a life-giving way, not because you are good or wonderful, but because that is what God has done. So, if we can shift our preoccupations, anxiety, and selfishness out of the way to put someone in touch with the possibility of God's healing, to that extent we are ourselves in touch with God's healing. So, if you gain your brother or sister, you gain God.

II.

If we ask how this literature contributes to any kind of contemporary understanding of Christian life together, the answer must lie in two of the words at the heart of that saying of Saint Anthony's with which we started—*life* and *win*. To find my own life is a task I cannot undertake without the neighbor; life itself is what I find in solidarity, and not only in a sense of togetherness (talking about solidarity can easily turn into no more than this) but in that will-ingness to put "on hold" the perspective I want to own and cling to and possess, so that something else may hap-pen through my presence and my words—the something else that is the announcing of the gospel. And *winning* is a word not about succeeding so that other people lose but about succeeding in connecting others with life-giving reality. Together, these words challenge us to think about common life in radical ways.

What if the real criteria for a properly functioning common life, for social existence in its fullness, had to do with this business of connecting each other with life-giv-ing reality, with the possibility of reconciliation or whole-ness? What if the deepest threat to life together were standing in the way of another person's discovery of wholeness by an insistent clinging to self-justification? Our success (if we still want to use that not very helpful word) would be measurable only in the degree to which those around us were discovering a way to truth and life, and since we are not all that likely to know much about this simply on external grounds, we might never know anything at all about our success. We'd only know the struggle and weakness out of which we attempted to speak to each other; beyond that, who knows? We could be confident only in God's unfailing presence with us for forgiveness and in God's unceasing summons to us to act for the reconciliation of others.

So a properly functioning human group, doing what human groups under God are meant to do, would also be one where we were engaged in learning quite intensively about the pressures that make us run away from this presence. We should need to be developing some very well-tuned antennae for the varieties of competitiveness that take us over and for the ways in which we assume, secretly or openly, that success is always about someone else's loss. This prompts some uncomfortable thoughts about the sorts of disagreement we are so used to in the church. Inevitably, we think in terms of winning and losing: this or that controversy that must be resolved in accordance with God's will so that we prevail in God's name. It isn't that the desert tradition knows nothing of controversy, of course; these documents come to us from an age compared with which many of our squabbles are pretty tea partyish. It is simply that they leave us with the question of whether any particular victory in the constant and supposedly invigorating life of debate leaves some people more deeply alienated from God—and the nastier question of what we are going to do about it if that is so.

The church is a community that exists because something has happened that makes the entire process of self-justification irrelevant. God's truth and mercy have appeared in concrete form in Jesus and, in his death and resurrection, have worked the transformation that only

God can perform, told us what only God can tell us: that he has already dealt with the dreaded consequences of our failure, so that we need not labor anxiously to save ourselves and put ourselves right with God. The church's rationale is to be a community that demonstrates this decisive transformation as really experienceable. And since one of the chief sources of the anxiety from which the gospel delivers us is the need to protect our picture of ourselves as right and good, one of the most obvious characteristics of the church ought to be a willingness to abandon anything like competitive virtue (or competitive suffering or competitive victimage, competitive tolerance or competitive intolerance or whatever). The church points to the all-sufficiency of Christ when it is full of people whose concern is not to separate others from the hope of reconciliation and life by their fears and obsessions. A healthy church is one in which we seek to stay connected with God by seeking to connect others with God, one in which we "win God" by converting one another, and convert one another by our truthful awareness of frailty. And a church that is living in such a way is the only church that will have anything *different* to say to the world; how deeply depressing if all the church offered were new and better ways to succeed at the expense of others, reinstating the scapegoat mechanisms that the cross of Christ should have exploded once and for all.[18]

III.

The desert monastics have very little to say about theories of the atonement—apparently very little to say even about Jesus for quite a lot of the time. But they are speaking about and living out something that only begins to make sense in the context of the gospel, and we *are* reminded of what they actually read and thought about each day, as in the story of Macarius and Theopemptus. At the center of practically all they have to say is Christ's own command not to be afraid. Death to the neighbor, refusing to judge, the freedom to ask, like Abba Joseph, "Who am I?"—all of this is about freedom from fear.

The desert community tells the church, then and now, that its job is to be a fearless community, and it shows us some of the habits we need to develop in order to become fearless, habits of self-awareness and attention to each other, grounded in the pervasive awareness of God that comes from constant exposure to God in Bible reading and prayer. Put it in this way, we ought to be able to see why it is a total misreading of the desert literature to think that it's all about tolerance and niceness. Not judging anyone sounds at first like a very contemporary thing, the nonjudgmental attitude that so well fits a postmodern reluctance to identify any absolute rights and wrongs, truths and falsehoods. But the desert is about the struggle for truth or it is nothing. "God will forgive; that's his job," said a famous eighteenth-century cynic. The desert fathers and mothers are no less sure that God will forgive, but they know with equal certainty that for us to *receive* that forgiveness in such a way that our lives will be changed is a lifetime's work requiring the most relentless monitoring of our selfish and lazy habits of thinking and reacting.

We have to be strenuous yet relaxed. We certainly know how to talk about being strenuous, how to portray Christian life as a struggle, a drama, in which we're called to heroic achievement and endurance, and we know how to talk about being relaxed, relying on God's mercy when we fail and not taking things too seriously. But it's far from easy to see how we can hold the two together. We can imagine the tightly strung pitch of effort, the slackness of relaxation: how are both possible at once?

The desert teachers encourage us in many ways to expect the worst of ourselves. From Anthony onward, they tell us that we must expect trials to the very end[19] and even that the apparent ending of trial or fantasy or distraction is a dangerous thing.[20] We need to be aware of our fragility and never to stop weeping for it. Another frequent type of story in the literature is of a younger monk saying to an elder, in effect, "Haven't you earned your passage to heaven by now? Your asceticism is so great, your penance so ardent, your wisdom so obvious." And the older man will reply, "If I had three lifetimes, I still couldn't shed enough tears for my sins."[21] In a well-known ascetical treatise of Saint John Climacus of Mount Sinai, we read things about the need for penance that can freeze the blood of a liberal modern believer. What is hard for us to grasp is that the desert monks know with utter seriousness the cost to them of their sin and selfishness and vanity, yet know that God will heal and accept. That they know the latter doesn't in any way diminish the intensity with which they know the former, and their knowledge of the former is what gives them their almost shocking tenderness toward other sinners.

They are not, in their tears and penances, trying to make up their debt to God. They know as well as any Christian that this is paid once and for all by the mercy that arrives in advance of all our repentance. They simply want to be sure that this assurance of mercy does not make them deceive themselves about why mercy is needed, by themselves and others. If they continue with this awareness of the sinful and needy self, it is so that they will understand the tears and self-hatred of others and know how to bring them to Christ by their unqualified acceptance and gentleness. So the strenuousness is in the effort to keep before our eyes the truth of our condition; the relaxedness is in the knowledge of a mercy that cannot ever be exhausted. It could be summed up in the formula of a great Anglican monastic reformer of the nineteenth century, R. M. Benson, who believed he should have "a heart of stone towards myself, a heart of flesh toward others, a heart of flame toward God"; though we should be careful not to take the "heart of stone toward myself" as meaning some kind of passionate self-loathing rather than the merciless honesty that Benson, like the desert teachers, has in mind.

The truth is that we will only understand the balance of severity and confidence, the strenuous and the relaxed, in the context of the common life. Every believer must have an urgent concern for the relation of the neighbor to Christ, a desire and willingness to be the means by which Christ's relation with the neighbor becomes actual and transforming. But that urgent concern arises from the sense in *myself* of the cost and grief involved in separation from life in God, the self-awareness of frailties and failures that I cannot overcome for and by myself. I have, by God's grace, learned as a member of the Christian community what is the nature of God's mercy, which does not leave me to overcome my sin by my own effort, so I have something to say to the fellow-sufferer who does not know where to look for hope. And what I have to say depends utterly on my willingness not to let go of that awareness of myself that reminds me where I start each day—not as a finished saint but as a needy person still struggling to grow.

Sin is healed by solidarity, by identification. Its power is shattered by the act of God in Christ; that act creates the community of Christ's body in which we live, ultimately, only through each other. This helps, too, to make sense of the varying attitudes of the desert fathers and mothers to physical self-denial. The literature has examples of real extremes of asceticism, and it has instances of very relaxed attitudes to penance and discouragement of excessive zeal. Different people need different disciplines to keep them attentive: the disaster is when one kind of discipline is either practiced as a means of superiority or imposed on others without attention. The whole purpose of any kind of ascesis is to challenge and overcome in ourselves whatever makes us an obstacle to the connection between God and the neighbor. So we should expect variety and should beware of any pressure to uniform severity, but the implication is also that we should beware of any slackening of the underlying watchfulness in regard to the self and its delusions. Not for nothing does the word *nepsis*, watchfulness, become the key concept of later monasticism in the Christian East.[22] If we trivialize the depth of our human need for God, we shall never be instruments to others of reconciliation. If we are unaware in ourselves of this need, because we have no disciplines for recognizing who and what we are, the church becomes ineffective.

Some of the most interesting recent research on desert monasticism has been on the significance and understanding of common life among the first generations of monks.[23] The surface pattern of "running" or "fleeing" from human contact is much more nuanced than it seems. What is to be learned in the desert is clearly not some individual technique for communing with the divine but the business of becoming a means of reconciliation and healing for the neighbor. You "flee" to the desert not to escape neighbors but to grasp more fully what the neighbor is—the way to life for *you*, to the degree that you put yourself at their disposal in connecting them with God. The unusual community that is the desert monastery of the first generation is not meant to be an alternative to human solidarity but a radical version of it that questions the priorities of community in other contexts. And this remains the most important function of any monastic community today—for the church and the wider world alike.

The figures we have begun to meet in the desert are not a set of interchangeable monastic clones but highly distinctive personalities. The ideal of finding your life by putting yourself at the service of another person's reconciliation with God could conceivably be taken as a recommendation simply to stop *having* a self in the ordinary sense. Of course, this is a misreading, but you can see why it might look plausible. Here we have to be reminded of why the desert fathers and mothers valued self-awareness. To be a real agent for God to connect with the neighbor in the way we have been thinking about, each of us needs to know the specific truth about himself or herself. It's no good just saying to yourself "I'm a sinner" in general terms. The specific facts of your experience may or may not be helpful to another—you should not assume that you always need to share the details, but you need to know them yourself. To be the means of reconciliation for another within the body of Christ, you must be consciously yourself, knowing what has made you who you are. And knowing what your typical problems, your brick walls are, and especially what your gifts are.

This doesn't mean that every Christian has to have the same kind of self-consciousness—that would be to destroy the whole point. People know themselves in very diverse ways and express that self-knowledge very differently. A child may be the means of connecting a person with God, as may an adult with severe learning difficulties; it isn't that holiness is the preserve of literary and educated self-awareness. But for anyone at all, even the child, even the person with a "handicap," the capacity to have some kind of loving and truthful *look* at himself or herself is surely part of the human presence that is there—to be aware at some level of one's distinctiveness, and to be aware of it as being in the hands of God.

The neighbor is our life; to bring connectedness with God to the neighbor is bound up with our own connection with God. The neighbor is our death, communicating to us the death sentence on our attempts to settle who we are in our own terms and to cling to what we reckon as our achievements. "Death is at work in us and life in you," as Saint Paul says (2 COR. 4:12), anticipating the themes of the desert. He is writing about how the apostle's suffering and struggle make the life of Christ visible in such a way that others are revived in hope. And it is as others discover this life in hope that we receive it too, the gift we could not have expected as we, with such difficulty and reluctance and intermittent resentment, had to learn to let go of our own lives and learn how to attend in love to the neighbor. We love with God when and only when we are the conduit for God's reconciling presence with the person next to us. It is as we connect the other with the source of life that we come to stand in the place of life, the place cleared and occupied for us by Christ.

2.

Silence and Honey Cakes

I.

Spiritual tourism did not take long to develop in fourth- and fifth-century Egypt. Travelers would come from far to see one or other of the great old men, and the desert literature has no shortage of stories about some of the surprises they encountered. It is one of the most memorable of these stories that gives its title to this chapter.

> A certain brother came to see Abba Arsenius at Scetis. He arrived at the church and asked the clergy if he could go and visit Abba Arsenius. "Have a bite to eat," they said, "before you go to see him." "No," he replied, "I shan't eat anything until I have met him." Arsenius's cell was a long way off, so they sent a brother along with him. They knocked on the door, went in, and greeted the old man, then sat down; nothing was said. The brother from the church said, "I'll leave you now; pray for me."

But the visitor didn't feel at ease with the old man and said, "I'm coming with you." So off they went together. Then the visitor said, "Will you take me to see Abba Moses, the one who used to be a highwayman?" When they arrived, Abba Moses welcomed them happily and enjoyed himself thoroughly with them until they left.

The brother who had escorted the visitor said to him, "Well, I've taken you to see the foreigner and the Egyptian; which do you like better?" The Egyptian [Moses] for me!" he said. One of the fathers overheard this and prayed to God saying, "Lord, explain this to me. For your sake, one of these men runs from human company and for your sake the other receives them with open arms." The two large boats floating on the river were shown to him. In one of them sat Abba Arsenius and the Holy Spirit of God in complete silence. And in the other boat was Abba Moses, with the angels of God: they were all eating honey cakes.[1]

What could put more clearly the sense of the distinctiveness of vocations? This is why inattention is such a problem in the context of the desert communities, insen-

sitivity to the real differences in people's callings and gift-
ings. Silence and honey cakes are not competing achievements. Such anxiety as there is in the story belongs with
the visitor, who can't quite cope with Arsenius's austerity
(as many other stories indicate, he was notorious for his
silences[2])—and with the eavesdropping monk, who can't
see how to reconcile the two styles; there is no hint that
Moses or Arsenius lost any sleep over their diversity.

The same concerns appear in a brief anecdote associated with Anthony himself:

> It was revealed to Abba Anthony in the desert
> that there was a person living in the city who
> was spiritually his equal. He was a physician;
> whatever he had beyond what he needed he
> gave to the poor, and every day he sang the
> Trisagion [the threefold liturgical prayer "Holy
> God, holy and strong, holy and immortal, have
> mercy on us] with the angels.[3]

Other versions begin with a "great old man" actually
asking God if there is anyone who is as holy as he is, and
being taken in the spirit to Alexandria to see some very
ordinary person doing a very ordinary job. There is no
notion of a vocation that is superior in the abstract, only
the attempt to identify those who become holy by doing
what they alone are called by God to do. There are no

standardized forms of holiness, no holiness that is imper-
sonal. Each person brings something different of the en-
terprise of desert life. Sin is always sin, but people live with
different degrees of pressure and temptation.

> A brother asked one of the fathers, "Are you
> defiled by having wicked thoughts?" There
> was a discussion about this, and some said
> "Yes" and others "No." The brother went to a
> very experienced old man and asked him
> about what was being discussed. The old man
> said, "What is required of each person is regu-
> lated according to his capacity."[4]

No one knows for sure how hard temptation might
bear on another. It is like Augustine exclaiming in exas-
perated compassion, when faced with Pelagian teachers
who insisted that all sin was a fully conscious rejection of
God, "Most sins are committed by people weeping and
groaning."[5] A temptation that might seem trivial to you
could be crushing to another; an obsession that haunts
you day and night may be incomprehensible to someone
else. This is why it is dangerous to demand that everyone
be the same kind of ascetic; everyone comes from a different past, with different memories and abilities. We
hear about a monk who complained to an older monk
that Abba Arsenius was not renowned for physical ascet-

icism. The older monk asks the complainer what he had done before becoming a monk. He had worked as a shepherd, sleeping on the ground, eating sparse meals of gruel, while Arsenius had been tutor to the imperial family and slept between sheets of silk. In other words, the simplicity of desert life represented no very great change for the censorious observer but a different world for Arsenius.[6]

Indeed, Arsenius was famous not for physical self-denial but for silence, and if there *is* one virtue almost universally recommended in the desert, it is this. Silence somehow reaches to the root of our human problem, it seems. You can lead a life of heroic labor and self-denial at the external level, refusing the comforts of food and sleep, but if you have not silence—to paraphrase Saint Paul—it will profit you nothing. There is a saying in the desert literature describing Satan,[7] or the devils in general, as the greatest of ascetics: the devil does not sleep or eat—but this does not make him holy. He is still imprisoned in that fundamental lie which is evil. And our normal habits of speech so readily reinforce that imprisonment. Again and again the desert teachers point out where speech can lead us astray. One of the rare occasions when something positive is said about the great but controversial monastic theologian Evagrius in the *Sayings of the Desert Fathers* is when he is depicted as accepting humbly the rebuke of another monk and keeping silence in a debate.[8] Abba

Pambo is represented as refusing to speak to the visiting archbishop of Alexandria: "If he is not edified by my silence, he will not be edified by my speech," says the old man, unanswerably.[9] (Archbishops are regarded with healthy suspicion in most of this literature.) Words help to strengthen the illusions with which we surround, protect, and comfort ourselves; without silence, we will not get any closer to knowing who we are before God.

The quality of our silence is a real issue. There is a silence that is poisonous and evil. That is when someone is being silenced by someone else. This is a silence that is resentful because it is the bottling up of feelings that one cannot trust either oneself to express or anyone else to listen to. The Simon and Garfunkel song from the sixties, "The Sound of Silence," depicts people being silenced or bottling up what they cannot say. Their words fall away into a malignant and destructive silence of helplessness and falsity, and idolatry arises. That is the exact opposite of the silence we are considering, and we need to know how to tell the difference.

There is an affirming silence that is attentive, focused, and that comes out of peace, not anger, from fullness, not woundedness. (Or perhaps from both.) There is a silence that speaks of both fullness and woundedness. Our freedom to be silent in that way reflects our freedom from resentment and the struggle for power. That is why authentic silence is so difficult. The freedom to be silent in this way indicates an affirmation, the great Yes to life in freedom from anger, power struggle, and resentment.

In conversation, in teaching, or in a pastoral relationship, we also need to know how to read silences. There can be a silence that indicates "I am giving up here. I do not know how to relate. I do not know how to respond. I feel powerless." My own greatest pastoral disasters always seem to have arisen when I have somehow silenced somebody so the person has not been able to speak and has felt overwhelmed or disempowered. There can be silence in a teaching relationship that says, "Oh well. You know all the answers, why should I bother to say anything?" We need fine discernment because sometimes in the pastoral and teaching relationships there is another kind of silence. Alongside my memories of pastoral disaster, I can also remember times when I have understood that I did not need to say much at all and nor did the other person. That is right silence.

Silence is letting what there is be what it is. In that sense it has to do profoundly with God: the silence of simply being. We experience that at times when there is nothing we can say or do that would not intrude on the integrity and the beauty of that being.

In a second-century Christian writing, the so-called protogospel of James, there is a description of the moment when Christ is born. Joseph has gone off to find a midwife. Mary is back in the cave and Joseph is walking through the fields toward the village. And suddenly everything stops. Then, Joseph says, he saw a shepherd in the field dipping his bread in a pot and the bread arrested halfway to his mouth. He saw a bird in heaven stopping in its flight. Just for a moment everything stands still. And then things go on and Joseph realizes that it has happened.

We have to be careful about the risk of modernizing the desert tradition in a shallow way: it sounds wonderful when we are told that the path of silence and asceticism is all about self-discovery, because we are most of us deeply in love with the idea of self-expression—and discovering the "true self" so as to express it more fully. That is the burden of hundreds of self-help books. But for the desert fathers and mothers, the quest for truth can be frightening, and they know how many strategies we devise to keep ourselves away from the real thing. They arc familiar with the idea that to discover ourselves, all we really need is for other people to go away—or at least to fall into the parts we have written for them and not try to change us or interfere with our plans. The essentially corporate character of this monastic self-discovery is fundamental to the therapy it provides. Our life is with the neighbor. And if everybody else were indeed taken away, we would not actually have a clue about who we "really" were. The sense in which we also need to be independent of the judgments of others is of course equally significant.

The American writer Annie Dillard, one of the most exhilarating and fresh writers about the natural world and human experience in the last few decades, has a short book called *The Writing Life*, which provides a very candid and very funny account of the process of creative writing. She is totally honest about the myriad ways in which we try to avoid the actual horrible business of writing when we have set aside time for it, and she identifies, too, how work in progress "goes wild" if we leave it overnight, so that we don't know how to start again.[10] And we are afraid to carry on because we know—if we are really trying to write properly—that honest self-expression is the hardest thing in the world; it needs self-scrutiny and self-abandonment.

> The part you must jettison is not only the best-written part; it is also, oddly, that part which was to have been the very point.[11]

What you thought mattered—what you thought was truest to the *real you*—often turns out to be empty and dishonest. You have to keep asking and keep looking; no wonder we hate it and find every excuse for not getting on with it. There is a faint echo of T. S. Eliot's "What you thought you came for / is only a shell, a husk of meaning" or Rilke's "archaic statue'" in his poem of that name, telling you that there are no places to hide and instead "you must change your life." Your surface ideas have to go, and so does the notion that you can produce something by an act of will. In fact, as a famous sculptor once said to his students, *will* has no part in the creative process. The use of the will is simply to keep you at it—but it doesn't deliver the product, because you don't yet know what you most truthfully want.

Some of this is put startlingly in a saying of the desert father John the Dwarf:

> We have put aside the easy burden, which is self-accusation, and weighed ourselves down with the heavy one, self-justification.[12]

This is very counterintuitive but entirely in tune with what is being said about the self in general. Self-justification is the heavy burden because there is no end to carrying it; there will always be some new situation where we need to establish our position and dig a trench for the ego to defend. But how on earth can you say that self-accusation is a light burden? We have to remember the fundamental principle of letting go of our fear. Self-accusation, honesty about our failings, is a light burden because whatever we have to face in ourselves, however painful is the recognition, however hard it is to feel at times that we have to start all over again, we know that the burden is already known and accepted by God's mercy. We do not have to create, sustain, and save ourselves; God has done, is doing, and will do all. We have only to be still, as Moses says to the people of Israel on the shore of the Red Sea (Exod. 14:14).

An old joke says that the Englishman takes pride in being a self-made man, thereby relieving God of a fearful responsibility. (Of course, the urge to be creators of ourselves is not restricted to any one nation or class.) Whenever we give over our energies to self-justification, we set our feet on this road to the impossible. No wonder John the Dwarf calls it the heavier burden. We fear the other kind of burden because carrying it means that certain things are decisively out of our control and we can only respond in trust or faith. Jesus says in Matthew 11:30 that his yoke is easy—and the saying of John the Dwarf is undoubtedly meant to call this text to mind—but we can hardly forget that Jesus also tells us to pick up and carry the cross. To see—to feel—the cross as a light load is the impossible possibility of faith: letting our best-loved pictures of ourselves and our achievements die, trying to live without the protections we are used to, *feels* like hell most of the time. But the real hell is never to be able to rest from the labors of self-defense. It is only very slowly indeed that we come to see why the bearing of the cross is a deliverance, not a sentence, why the desert fathers and mothers could combine relentless penance with confidence and compassion.

There is a saying ascribed to Isidore the Priest warning that "of all evil suggestions, the most terrible is the prompting to follow your own heart."[13] Once again, the modern reader will be taken aback. "Follow what your heart says" is part of the standard popular wisdom of our day, like "following your dream." Are we being told to suspect our deepest emotions and longings, when surely we have learned that we have to listen to what's deepest in us and accept and nurture our real feelings? But the desert monastics would reply that, left to ourselves, the search for what the heart prompts is like peeling an onion; we are not going to arrive at a pure and simple set of inclinations. In the matter of self-examination, as in others, "the truth" is rarely "pure" and never "simple." The desert means a stepping back from the great system of collusive fantasy in which I try to decide who I am, sometimes try to persuade you to tell me who I am (in accord, of course, with my preferences), sometimes use God as a reinforcement for my picture of myself, and so on and on. The "burden" of self-accusation, the suspicion of what the heart prompts, this is not about an inhuman austerity or self-hatred but about the need for us all to be coaxed into honesty by the confidence that God can forgive and heal. Henri de Lubac, one of the most outstanding Roman Catholic theologians of the twentieth century, put it with a clarity and brevity very hard to improve upon: "It is not sincerity, it is truth which frees us.... To seek sincerity above all things is perhaps, at bottom, not to want to be transformed." He has also observed that "psychology alone is not suited, at least in the most subtle cases, to discern the difference between the authentic and the sham."[14] Like the desert teachers, he warns us against easy assumptions about the natural wisdom of the human heart.

If the heart contains the love of God, one may wonder where is the danger of being guided by it? It is confusing on the surface, but there is something intelligible behind this contradiction. It was Abba Isidore who expressed strong reservations about being guided by the heart. These reservations have to do with listening to what you *think* are the promptings of your feelings. He wants us to be clear that listening to these promptings is not a guarantee of getting it right. "How can I be wrong if I am so sincere?" is not a Christian principle.

If we can get to the true depth of the heart, what we find there is the echo of God's creative word. Each one of us is a unique kind of echo of God. This does not mean that if we uncovered our deepest consciousness, we would find the Ten Commandments written there. It is that we are, by the very nature of our humanity, naturally *attuned* to the reality of God. Our task in growing up in the life of the spirit is to try to recover that attunement. I think of that, for example, when I listen to Bach, who somehow does a great deal more theology in a few bars of music than most do in many words.

Deep down we are attuned to God, but we have jarred the harmonies in various ways. We are out of tune. The trouble then is that what we often listen to is the out-of-tuneness, the habits of self-protection and self-regard. If that is what listening to the heart means, forget it. That is just canonizing what we *think* is going on in us. We have a lot of self-knowledge to acquire before we can truly listen to the heart.

God alone will tell me who I "really" am, and he will do so only in the lifelong process of bringing my thoughts and longings into his presence without fear and deception. The central importance in desert practice of "manifesting your thoughts" to an elder is only partly about receiving good advice, getting your problems sorted out; it is more deeply about how the elder "stands in" for a truth that is greater than any human presence. The novice's fugues and chains of fantasy or obsession are poured out, sometimes receiving only the barest of acknowledgments and very little we would think of as counseling, but the job has been done, because the novice has been learning not to "follow" the heart in the sense of taking what he discovers inside himself for granted but to see the heart in all of its complex, yearning, frightened actuality and to find words for it. When there is no manifestation of thoughts, there is no progress, as so many of the narratives make plain: "Nothing makes the enemy happier," says John the Dwarf, "than those who do not manifest their thoughts."[15] Defenselessness before the elder who represents God: that is the key to growth for the monks and nuns of the desert. It is not simply a matter of submitting to the authority of an elder to be told what to do. When the novice approaches the elder and says, in the usual formula, "Give me a word," he or she is not asking for either a command or a solution but for a communication that can be received as a stimulus to grow into fuller life. It is never a theoretical matter, and the elders are scathing about those who simply want something to discuss.[16] "The desert produced healers, not thinkers," in the fine formulation of John Chryssavgis.[17] The novice, in approaching the elder, both to manifest thoughts and to ask for a saving word, is becoming vulnerable, and that is the heart of the transformation that, as Father de Lubac says, we are by no means sure we really want, if that is what it costs.

II.

Once again, we can think of what the church would be like if it were indeed a community not only where each saw his or her vocation as primarily to put the neighbor in touch with God but where it was possible to engage each other in this kind of quest for the truth of oneself, without fear, without the expectation of being despised or condemned for not having a standard or acceptable spiritual life. There would need to be some very fearless people around, which is why a church without some quite demanding forms of long-term spiritual discipline—whether in traditional monastic life or not—is going to be a frustrating place to live.

It is also going to be a deeply ineffective witness to the society around. Some of the themes we have been thinking about in this chapter bear quite directly on the hidden and not-so-hidden crises of our civilization. We live in a society that is at once deeply individualist and deeply conformist; the desert fathers and mothers manage to be neither, and they suggest to us that the church's calling likewise is to avoid both of these pitfalls. Think for a moment about this paradox of individualism and conformity. We are fascinated by the power of the individual will and intensely committed to maximizing this power, the power to shape and to define a person's life through the greatest possible number of available choices. The political philosopher Raymond Plant recently noted that religion can be quite acceptable in such an environment because it represents another choice that consumers can make in shaping their lives; it enriches the range of the market.[18] The religious person in this context might well reverse what Jesus says to his friends in the Gospel of John: "*We* have chosen *you*, so that we may have the life we desire."

And the problem is that we are actually so naive about choices, forgetting that this world of maximal choice is heavily managed and manipulated. The rebellious teen-ager has a ready-made identity to step into, professionally serviced by all the manufacturers who have decided what a rebellious teenager should look like; advertising stan-dardizes our dreams. Our choices are constantly chan-neled into conformist patterns, and when we try to escape, there are often standard routes provided by the very same market. ("Don't be like the crowd!" says the ad-vertisement that is trying to persuade you to do the same as all the other customers it's targeting.)

The desert fathers and mothers might say to young people today, "What's the hurry?" They would be amazed to see the way our culture prizes speed. They might say that the hurried urgency to possess and consume is an index of falsehood and a misunderstanding of the kind of being you are. It is all right to take time. Only in taking time can you realize how much more you are than an *in-dividual*. By taking time you are built by the character of the world you are in and the people around you. Wittgen-stein said that the most important thing one philosopher can say to another is to "take your time."

Young people do not become mature religious peo-ple of faith unless they have been helped to experience their own humanity. As a theologian, I would say this means being taught to experience their humanity as cre-ated and loved and healed. You may not necessarily say all of that to them, but that is the basis on which you move.

However, too often we think religious education is about putting in more information. Instead, religious education, when it is doing its job of "educating the spirit," has to be the conveying—in all aspects of the educational environment—of the "peaceful worthwhileness" of each person. Individuals as they are at rest are worthwhile, just as they are. From that God will move. God will create. God will change. Particularly religious education in the primary school must focus on the messages to the child about that peaceful worthwhileness. There is no sight more wonderful than a meeting hall with three or four hundred children sitting in prayerful silence. I have seen it and know it can be done. They are free to be silent. No one is threatening them, but they are being told "You have room just to sit and breathe." For the future, conveying this sense of peaceful worthiness is much more fundamental to religious formation than just communicating religious information.

Often we think religious education is about bolting on some more technology to what we have already got, and putting in more information. Too often, the whole atmosphere of school and college pushes tense, driven messages of anxiety about the need to fill in all the open spaces. You must never waste time, is the message. The arts, music and drama, even sports, are pushed to the margins except when promoted as another form of competition. In such an atmosphere, whatever you say in spiritual or religious education, you are actually breeding atheists, because you are creating a shrunken humanity.

III.

The longing for individuality, the pressure to conform, the fascination with the will and the reduction of the will to choices in the market: these are some of the knottiest tangles in our contemporary world. And to understand them fully, perhaps we need a bit more theology than we usually think about. The Russian Orthodox writer Vladimir Lossky based much of his theology around the controversial claim that you need to distinguish with absolute clarity between the individual and the person: the person is what is utterly unique, irreducible to a formula, made what it is by the unique intersection of the relationships in which it's involved. This is obviously grounded in what we believe about the "persons" of the Holy Trinity, about the way *God* is personal. However, the individual is just *this* rather than *that* example of human nature, something essentially abstract. It can be spoken of in clichés and generalities. It is one possible instance, among others, of the way general human capacities or desires or instincts operate.[19]

The person is the completely unique and therefore mysterious core of every human agent. To be a person is simply to be distinct. The person is completely distinct and yet also exists only in relationship. The realm of the personal is that realm in which what *I* am as unique, mysterious, and distinctive comes into relation with what is unique and mysterious and distinctive in *you*. Each of us then makes the other even more unique and mysterious and distinctive in the process.

Individuals are repeatable and, in some ways, replaceable. Persons are unique and irreplaceable. Remember the song "Clementine" and the sad fate of its heroine. In its last verse it says, "So I kissed her little sister and forgot my Clementine." That is what *personal* being is not about. Little sisters do not substitute for Clementine. No one of us substitutes for another, because we are not "repeatable instances." I can drop a glass on the floor. It breaks and someone will replace it. It does not much matter. But with the personal, it matters a lot. With every person there is one way in which that person can show the life of God—and that person only. The life of God is reflected in a distinct history and a distinct set of responses and creative engagements in the world.

The difference between the person and the individual is that the individual in this framework simply means one example of a type. For instance, I can pick up an individual glass. There are lots of glasses with varying features, but you can describe them as variations on a single theme. They are examples of a general substance or nature, a type of life or reality. And although they are different from each other, they are, in principle, reducible to one basic definition. Lossky says that when we talk about the personal, we are trying to say something more than that. The person is more than just an example of a type. And a person in Christ, the holy person in a particular way, is more than that too. There is no general type of Christian holiness. There is an infinite variety of different relationships to Jesus Christ, which also become relationships with each other.

I love telling people at confirmation services that when I ask the Holy Spirit to come into their lives in this sacrament, I am saying that there is something you can do which nobody else can in the life of the community. I ask them not to forget that, because it means that you need the church and the church needs you.

For Lossky it is very important that the church is a community of persons. He says there are two errors into which it can fall. The church can be a community of individuals, that is, a people who are making a concordat or compromise with each other to live together: "We do not really quite know how much we have in common, but we can manage somehow." We draw up an agreement so that we can cope. Lossky sees this as an error of Protestantism. He also says that an error of Catholicism is to treat the church as a solid mass, almost undifferentiated, with little room for either the individual or the person. And not surprisingly, he says Eastern Orthodoxy has got the right balance, because it is interested in the person.

So the exercise of choice in the usual modern sense belongs with this natural, individual order of being rather than with the truly personal. In making a choice, any choice, one is exercising a capacity common to all, one expression of human wanting. The fact of having choices is a fact about human nature as we experience it, but it is not this that constitutes us as persons. We may like to think that the choices we make are the distinctive thing about us, what tells us and others who we are, but as Lossky and other Eastern Christian writers of recent decades see it,[20] these may be some of the least distinctive, even the least interesting, things about us. We might even say that the mature human being is not the one who has the most choices available but the one who apparently makes the fewest choices, who freely does what he or she *is*, without self-consciousness or self-assertion, without anxious fretting about what would be more authentic.

We can only really make sense of this, as expounded by Lossky and his followers, if we think about the supremely free and supremely distinctive human being Jesus. There was a certain amount of argument historically about the character and extent of Jesus's free will as a human being: could he, under the great pressure of Gethsemane, for example, have decided to escape, to do something else? If the answer is no, how can we say that he was really "tempted as we are"? If the answer is yes, does that not make nonsense of our belief that in every moment his human nature was fully and unequivocally united with God? Not long after the age of the first desert fathers and mothers, the Eastern church was violently divided over the question of whether we should say that Jesus had one will or two: did there exist in Jesus both a divine will and a human one, or only one will that was some sort of compound of the two? The latter option assumed that if there was only one *person* in Jesus (as the official formula said), there must be only one will. But after a long and bitter struggle, the church decided that we should speak of two wills, because there are two natures in Christ.

It sounds appallingly abstruse to us, but in fact it is of the greatest relevance to the issues we are thinking about. To have a "will," for the Orthodox theologians of that era, was to have a set of dispositions that went with your nature: if this is the *kind* of being you are, this is the *kind* of thing you're likely to want. Choosing among the kinds of thing you're liable to want is on this account a "natural" activity. So, for Jesus in the garden of Gethsemane, the human will is active, and the human will wants to survive and rebels against the threat of not surviving. It can envisage the threat of death and envisage what might be needed to escape death. In a purely formal and abstract sense, it is able to "choose" to survive, because that is what human wills do.

But the human will is not the human person, and all this is quite abstract when considered apart from the person who activates the willing. There are no such things as wills that drift around in midair making decisions. Persons do the deciding, and when you have a person who is wholly self-consistent, whose identity is completely bound up with the calling to live in unreserved intimacy with God as Father, there is, as we say, *no* choice. Not because something external limits what's possible but because the person has such solid reality, such distinctive and reliable identity, that it will do what is consistent with being *that person*—and in the case of Jesus, this means doing what God requires for the salvation of the world. There may be turmoil at the level of feelings, a keen awareness of the cost, a shrinking from what is ahead, but there is no ultimate uncertainty. And this does not mean that Jesus is somehow spared the awfulness of human decision in the face of terrible risk and agony, only that *who he is* is what settles the matter once and for all. He is completely free to be himself, and it is unthinkable—and only abstractly possible—that he should refuse his calling (any human being in the abstract can say yes or no to anything). But this does not reduce his freedom. Instead it establishes what is the most important freedom of all.

This question was addressed by the great Anglican monastic theologian Herbert Kelly. When asked by one of his novices, "How do we know what the will of God is?" Kelly replied, "We do not. That is the joke." In fact, Kelly is right. We never know precisely what the will of God is. I remember wrestling once with a serious pastoral problem in the diocese and absolutely not knowing what to do. I can recall myself saying to God at the end of my evening prayers, "Look, just for once would you mind saying something? I would really like to know." Even knowing that that was not available, it is what we all want.

In addition to this, God leaves the question about his will to a process of discernment of our free will. The discernment goes like this: We have to choose between a number of courses of action. What course of action more fully resonates with the kind of life Christ lived and lives? What sort of action opens up more possibilities for God to work? Now, those are not questions that immediately yield an answer. But they are the stuff, the raw material of reflection. What course of action might be (even a little) more in tune with the life of Christ? And what opens, rather than closes, doors for God's healing, reconciling, forgiving, and creating work to go on? It may well be that in any given situation there simply is not a clear answer to those questions. But if they are the questions we are asking, then the very process of reflecting and discerning makes space in ourselves for the life of Christ and the creative movement of God. To the extent to which we truthfully and sincerely make that space, we are already in tune with the will of God. Even if we go on to make a mistake, we have not done it by shutting the door on God. We have done our best to leave room for God in the decision we made. To the degree we manage that, we really do (in some measure) God's will. We must simply leave God room and freedom to salvage our life from whatever mess our decision may bring with it.

The monastic theologians of the sixth century showed a good deal of interest in comparing the temptations of Jesus with other human temptations as part of the process of getting clear about how far a sense of the possibility of doing wrong already involved some kind of mental sin. For Jesus to have suffered real human temptation, he must have gone through some of the same mental processes as we do. And if he could be tempted yet not be held guilty, there must be some level in our minds and hearts where we can say, yes, we are aware of the possibility, even the attractive possibility, of wrongdoing, yet not be involved in a conscious refusal of God. The technicalities of doctrine about Christ do have a direct pastoral relevance for those who are tormented by guilt about what they cannot help. There comes a point where we deliberately welcome the image of wrongdoing and begin to put flesh on it in our imaginations, and that is when responsibility begins.[21] So we are encouraged to see Jesus as fully aware of the general possibilities of human nature, including the possibilities of betrayal, cowardice, and self-gratification, aware of those as part of his composition as a person with a human nature, yet not actively welcoming them, not saying yes to them, so that it still makes sense to describe him as without sin.

Perhaps part of the problem is that modern Western readers in particular are a bit inclined to romanticize struggle and tension. At least since Kant in the eighteenth century, there is a feeling that *really* good deeds are the ones we do with the most effort, after the biggest struggles. So our moral thinking has concentrated on the difficulties of decision making more than on the character that develops over a lifetime. But if we think of those people whose moral and spiritual integrity has mattered to us and made a difference to us, we will normally find that they are the ones whose behavior doesn't draw attention to how difficult it all is, how hard they're working to be good. They are people for whom there is a "naturalness" about what they do. They have become a particular kind of *person*, and that personal reality has begun to change the human nature they live in, has begun to make slightly different things seem the obvious focus of desire. Once again, some of the theology of the Orthodox Church gives us a clue: Jesus, because as a person he is one with the Word of God, in perfect communion with the Father, changes human nature by his personal loving surrender to God in every detail of his life and death. Those who live in him by grace are in the process of having *their* human nature changed as their personal relation with him develops; they are growing into what is always fully present and accomplished in him. Human nature as transformed by his divine freedom is becoming "second nature" to them.

So the saint isn't someone who makes you think, "That looks hard; that's a heroic achievement of will"—with the inevitable accompanying thought, "That's too hard for me"—but someone who makes you think, "How astonishing! Human lives can be like that, behavior like that can look quite natural," with perhaps the thought, "How can I find what they have found?" The lives of holy people are full of incidents that make it startlingly clear how extraordinary behavior can arise without any apparent effort in situations of extreme pressure. John Fisher, bishop of Rochester, who was to be executed for his refusal to approve Henry VIII's policies, was woken up on the morning of his execution to be told that the time for his beheading had been changed to a couple of hours later, and he responded by saying that in that case he would welcome the chance to go back to sleep for a bit. A few years later, the Protestant martyr John Bradford was asked on the morning of *his* execution whether he felt frightened or disturbed, and he replied that he had slept so soundly that he hadn't heard the noisy singing that he was told had gone on in the cell next door. More recently, there is the story of Saint Edith Stein, Carmelite sister and convert from Judaism. When the Gestapo caught up with her in Holland, she was greeted by the officer in charge with the usual "*Heil* Hitler!" She simply replied with the old monastic formula of greeting, "*Laudetur Jesus Christus,*" "Jesus Christ be praised."

These are all examples of what Lossky means by *personal* action. These are memorable, distinctive, even quirky reactions to situations, coming from people who are being wholly themselves but seem to have no individualist agenda. Thinking about them, we may come to see more clearly how to distinguish the personal from the merely individual, and why this is the kind of distinction we need if we are to understand fully what the desert fathers and mothers have to say about vocation and holiness. And this helps us also to see once more that the desert literature has some significant things to say to us about the kind of community the church is or could be or should be. A community of mere individuals is hardly a community at all: it's a place where egos are jostling for advantage, competing for much the same goods, held together by a reluctantly accepted set of rules to limit the damage. But a community of people who have all been educated into complete conformity, so all its members want what they are told to want and everyone marches in step, would certainly have its own problems. We would always be watching one another to check for unanimity, always conscious of being policed. Plenty of societies have been down this road in the course of the last century.

The church is meant to be supremely a community of persons in the sense that we've been thinking about. It is a place for distinctive vocations to be discovered in such a way that they are a source of mutual enrichment and delight, not threat. It is a place where real human difference is nourished. I don't just mean the obvious fact that the church has to be a place of welcome for all races and cultures but that it must know how to work with the grain of different personal gifts and histories. A healthy church is one where there is evident diversity in this respect and plenty of bizarre characters (the same thing has often been said about monastic communities, even if sometimes through gritted teeth). An unhealthy church is one in which unity has been reduced to a homogeneity of opinions and habits, so that certain styles of devotion, or certain expressions of what God means to this or that person, are frowned on. Virtue becomes identified with uncontroversial ordinariness, and there is a nervous cultural "sameness" in the way people talk, dress, and behave. And beware of thinking that this is a problem just of the political right or of the left or, in general, of "them" rather than us.

IV.

Arsenius and Moses represent irreducible differences of "tone" in their response to the call of God in the desert, but the attitude of the tradition conserved in this story is to ask, "Why is this a problem?" I use the word *tone* because it's often the case that the musical metaphor best captures what this implies for the life of the Christian community. Different voices, different instruments, but an intelligible and beautiful result. What has always to be remembered is that this is more than "letting a thousand flowers bloom." A church that is simply recognizing different *preferences* is stuck at the level of individualism; the real work has not yet been done, the work that is the discovery of God's call beyond the simplistic "listening to the heart" that we all too readily settle for. This is a work that takes protracted, committed time, which is why the church is so much involved in blessing lifelong commitments—marriage, ordination, monastic life—not as a way of saying that everyone has to be involved in one or more of these but to remind all baptized believers that, because of their baptism, they are bound to the patient, long-term discovery of what grace will do with them. And it is a work that requires the kind of vulnerability to each other that can only come with the building up of trust over time, and the kind of silence that brings our fantasy identities to judgment. It all comes around to "life and death with the neighbor," once more.

If the church can manage this rather difficult agenda, it will be what it should be, a powerful challenge to all kinds of human togetherness that seek to override the reality of the person—whether the subtle pressures of consumerism or the open tyranny of totalitarianism. It will also challenge some of our impulses to take a shortcut around the processes of real personal exchange—whether it is the seductive idea that you can save money in education by having fewer teachers and more computers or, more seriously, the ease with which we can learn to redescribe civilian casualties in war as "collateral damage." The church may not have detailed solutions to practical problems in such areas, but it has a right and duty to remind the society around of what is at risk in any such shortcuts.

In this light, what is an honest "spiritual life"? Perhaps we should say that it is one in which the taste for truth, rather than sincerity, has become inescapable. We don't know what we will be, what face God will show to us in the mirror he holds up for us on the last day, but we can continue to question our own (and other people's) strange preference for the heavy burden of self-justification, self-creation, and weep for our reluctance to become persons and to be transfigured by the personal communion opened for us by Jesus.

3.

Fleeing

I.

> It was said of Abba Theodore of Pherme that
> the three things he believed to be basic for
> everything were poverty, asceticism, and flight.[1]

The theme of fleeing recurs many times in the desert
literature, and at first sight it seems a way of speaking
about the sheer physical separation involved in going off
to the desert. Things are a little more complicated than
that. One of the primary traditions about Arsenius describes a divine voice instructing him when he is still "in
the world": "Flee from human company and you will be
saved,"[2] but a probably slightly later story attached to the
name of Macarius suggests that the early generations of
monks were well aware of the different levels at which
this sort of language could be used:

> Abba Isaiah asked Abba Macarius to give him
> a word. The old man said, "Flee from human

company." Abba Isaiah said, "But what does it
mean to flee from human company?" The old
man said, "It means sitting in your cell and
weeping for your sins."[3]

Certainly the desert fathers and mothers were in
flight from the social systems of their day, from the conformity and religious mediocrity of what they found elsewhere. But they were clearly not running away from
responsibility or from relationships; everything we have so
far been considering underlines that they were entering
into a more serious level of responsibility for themselves
and others and that their relationships were essential to the
understanding of their vocation. Flight, as this saying of
Macarius's suggests, is about denying yourself the luxury
of solving your problems by running away literally or
physically from them (sit in your cell) and about taking responsibility for your sins (weep). We might compare the
saying of Anthony to Poemen that "the great work for
anyone is to go on taking the blame for his own sins before God and to expect trials till his last breath."[4] To solve
the stress by *not* fleeing, by resorting to "human company,"
is to blur the sharp edges of responsibility and to imagine
that we can arrange our situation to our comfort—as if by
changing the furniture, or changing the scenery, we can
change our inner landscape. As if by talking to others and
manipulating their reaction to us we can soften or share

out the guilt we feel and fear. If someone has offended or hurt me, accused me of something, pointed out something I'd rather not recognize, the attractive way through is to talk to someone else and get that person to reassure me that I'm wonderful and (ideally) that my critic is not worth listening to. But this is as useful in the long term as drinking saltwater; I shall have to work very hard indeed at the silencing of the critical voice which can become an obsessional search for absolution. This again is the heavy burden of self-justification. The desert fathers say *flee*. Run from the company and comfort that will make us feel better but will equally involve us in a lifetime's frustration.

If we were really trying to put this in contemporary terms, we might say that we are being encouraged to flee from "projection"—from other people's projections onto us, ours onto them, our own inflated expectations of ourselves. In fact, if you look up *flight* in an index of the desert fathers, you'll find quite a variety of things to flee from, and all of them have something to do with what we might think of as projection. We must flee from "thoughts"—*logismoi* in Greek, a technical term in monastic literature for the chains of obsessional fantasy that can take over our inner life[5]—and from status and dignity,[6] and from speech.[7] "Don't take pleasure in human conversation" says Macarius,[8] very austerely, as it seems to us, but as we shall see, fleeing from words is something very central indeed to all of this.

This is all closely tied in with the theme of winning your neighbor. Our life is with our neighbor, and so we must withdraw from everything that helps to imprison the neighbor, which entails looking very hard at what we say to or about the neighbor. The vocation of each is personal and distinctive, so each must have the room to grow as God, not we, would have him or her do. Fleeing is keeping that critical edge in awareness of what we say, keeping that reverent distance from the intimate places of the other's heart or conscience. And one very specific form of "flight" that gives much food for thought and comes up in a number of stories has to do with other people's conviction about what we could and should usefully do for the church. For example, in the desert literature, ordination to the priesthood is frequently presented as a burden and temptation that has to be avoided. When John Cassian famously advised monks to flee from women and bishops,[9] he had in mind the most obvious danger of being in proximity to a bishop: they might end up getting ordained. Occasionally, a desert monk was ordained against his will or his better judgment: Theodore of Pherme was made a deacon but constantly avoided exercising his ministry, when necessary by running away.

> Time after time, the old men brought him
> back to Scetis saying, "Do not abandon your
> role as a deacon." Abba Theodore said to them,

```
*****************************************
        SAVE 20% OFF
       1 BOOK OR CD
    WHEN YOU SPEND $20 OR MORE

        SAVE 20% OFF
     1 BOOK AND 1 CD
    WHEN YOU SPEND $30 OR MORE
```

Discount applies to the list price.

Valid at Borders, 7/27 - 8/2/2006

Book barcode:

```
1 5 9 0 1 3 6 6 0 0 0 0 0 0 0 0 0
```

CD barcode:

```
1 5 9 0 1 3 6 7 0 0 0 0 0 0 0 0 0
```

POS: This is a programmed coupon. If
the purchase is $20 or more, just scan
one apropriate barcode. If the
purchase is $30 scan both barcodes.
Previous & online purchases and gift
cards do not count towards the $20 or
$30 thresholds. Not valid with other
coupons, sale pricing or standard
group discounts. Cash value .01 cent.
Not redeemable for cash. No copies
allowed. Any other use constitutes
fraud. One coupon percustomer per day.
X   X
STORE: 0199   REG: 05/11   TRAN#: 8551
SALE   07/27/2006   EMP: 00230
****

"Let me pray to God so that he may tell me
for sure whether I ought to function publicly
as a deacon in the liturgy." This is how he
prayed to God: "If it is your will that I should
stand in this place, make me sure of it." A pillar
of fire appeared to him, stretching from earth
to heaven, and a voice said, "If you can become like this pillar of fire, go and be a deacon." So he decided against it. He went to
church, and the brothers bowed to him and
said, "If you don't want to be a deacon, at least
administer the chalice." But he refused and
said, "If you do not leave me alone, I shall
leave here for good." So they left him in
peace.[10]

The temptation is to say that figures like this were
avoiding responsibility or setting impossibly high standards to justify their refusal of office. But a better reaction
would be to think first about why exactly ordination was
seen by them in so negative a way. Theodore sees it in
terms of the fiery pillar uniting earth and heaven, and we
might recall the powerful story of Abba Joseph, raising his
hands to heaven and the fingers streaming with fire.[11]
The monk's calling is to "become fire." What then is
Theodore's problem? It is the identification of this personal summons to "become fire" with a specific visible

role in the church—as if ordination involved some sort of attempt to lay hold of a destiny that would take a lifetime of prayer and watchfulness to grow into. For Theodore, to be a deacon would mean to lay claim to a spiritual whole-ness that it would be impossibly arrogant to assume for oneself. It's true that the church does not encourage us to understand every struggle over vocation to ordained min-istry in such terms, but it is a story that ought to make all ordained people uncomfortable, if only in its clear sugges-tion that exercising a public role in the church's worship involves standing in the furnace of divine action that unites earth and heaven. If we can't see that this is a dan-gerous place, we have missed something essential.

Much of the suspicion shown toward ordained min-istry is less complex—and it applies to many more people than just those wrestling with the possibilities of ordina-tion (which also suggests that there may be those other than bishops who can equally well be the carriers of dan-gerous opportunities). It has to do, certainly, with status, and so with expectation (projection once again). The or-dained person may be at risk because of the spiritually in-tense nature of the place where the person must stand and also at risk from the more prosaic but still spiritually dam-aging effects of hierarchy and deference. Some Christians are of course called to exercise public ministry. Yet the desert literature is never antisacramental or even anti-in-stitutional in the sense of trying to reinvent the church as

a community of perfect souls who are too spiritual to
need the ordinary means of grace. The fact remains that
the calling to monastic witness is not going to be compat-
ible with a life in which it is easy to be ensnared in the fantasies of others and caught up in an illusory position of
dignity. This is not by any means a problem restricted to
ordained ministry; it's about any position where one has a
clearly defined chance of "doing good" and earning a reputation and respect. The issue is not about whether or not
someone should assume his or her "proper" responsibilities in the church (or society, for that matter); the primary
responsibility in the desert, as we have seen, is for your
own and each other's growth and truthfulness before God.

The ambivalence about ordained ministry has to do
with the license that the ordained person has to *talk*—to
instruct, explain, exhort, even control. We have seen how
wary the desert teachers could be about professional theologians and thinkers, and there are plenty of stories about
the need to avoid both theoretical discussions and over-
confidence on theological questions.[12] Ordained persons
as professional talkers would hardly be likely to commend
themselves in such an environment. Fleeing from speech
is presented sometimes as the very climax of all flight, as
in a story of Macarius's:

> One day, as Abba Macarius was dismissing the
> gathering, he said to the brothers at Scetis,

"Flee, brethren!" One of the old men asked
him, "Where could we flee to that is farther
away than this desert?" Macarius put his finger
to his lips and said, "Flee that." And off he
went to his cell, shut the door, and sat down.[13]

It is a nicely vivid picture—the slightly jaded old
monk looking around the miles of sand and asking where
there is left to run to, and Macarius's immediate and elo-
quently simple gesture in reply. However physically remote we may be from the more obvious temptations,
there is always the damage that can be done by speech, by
the giving and receiving of doubtfully truthful perspectives, the half-hidden power games of our talking—including our talking (and writing) about spiritual matters.
Speech that is not centered upon the processes we have
been examining—the painful confrontation of inner confusion, the painstaking making of space for each other before God—is part of that system which, in another of
Macarius's sayings, makes us do stupid things,[14] the world
that does not know itself for what it is.

G. K. Chesterton, in his hymn "O God of Earth and
Altar," wrote of the "easy speeches / That comfort cruel
men"; and we could say that the concern of the desert fathers and mothers is to save us from easy speeches and
from the ultimate cruelty they encode, the destructiveness
of the lies we tell ourselves and each other about human-

ity. Remember Annie Dillard's observation that the part we have to discard in our writing is what we think is best—which is often what most easily fits our expectations. If we leave this without criticism, the process of writing will not have changed us as it should. We need to develop a ruthless eye for hidden weaknesses, to make things difficult for ourselves as we write.

> Lay out the structure you already have, x-ray it
> for a hairline fracture, find it, and think about
> it for a week or a year; solve the insoluble
> problem. [15]

That x-raying is very close indeed to the desert precepts about taking on the burden of self-accusation. In the desert, the insoluble problem is myself; the hairline fracture is the elusive but fatal element of self-regard, inattention to the neighbor, which threatens to leave me eternally broken and at odds with God and myself. Like the writer struggling to avoid the obvious and the easy, we run from what is offered to us by the "easy" bits of our own soul or imagination and the easy ways of garnering approval from others. "Why do you have to be so *difficult?*" people sometimes say to writers; the answer is that a lot of the time only being awkward saves you from being stupid and egotistical. Likewise, holy people are frequently difficult as well as exciting and inspiring. I don't mean simply temperamental or unpredictable: holy people can be these things too, like everyone else, but it is more that they are not easily reduced to a formula, not easily conscripted into being reliable supporters of a cause, not good party members. They are too preoccupied with the X-rays.

The person who has heard the same challenge as the desert fathers and mothers, then, is in flight from conformity—not to secure a freedom of individual expression (we've seen how that can be one of the greatest illusions), but for the sake of a genuinely personal community. Such persons will treasure silence not as a means of cutting themselves off from relationship but as a way of doing what T. S. Eliot (writing in the *Four Quartets* about the poet's job) described as "purifying the dialect of the tribe"—restoring a language for this personal community that is as free as it can be from the little games of control and evasion that take up so much room in the talking of most of us. It's worth remembering that when Jesus tells his disciples most fully who he is, many find it "a hard saying" (JOHN 6:60). He does not give them an easy formula but speaks so as to invite them to recognize him and to recognize their own deepest needs and their own deepest truth. He speaks in the context of a relationship in which truth can be uncovered for us, and his words are given to us to absorb and repeat so that we can speak for him to one another. Gradually—and by the gift of the Spirit—a

*If you wish to receive a copy of the latest Shambhala
Publications catalogue of books and to be placed on our
mailing list, please send us this card, or e-mail us at:
info@shambhala.com*

PLEASE PRINT

Book in which this card was found

NAME

ADDRESS

CITY & STATE

ZIP OR POSTAL CODE   COUNTRY
                                      (if outside U.S.A.)

E-MAIL ADDRESS

SHAMBHALA PUBLICATIONS, INC.

Mailing List
P.O. Box 308, Back Bay Annex
Boston, Massachusetts
02117

new language will emerge for the new community of disciples: a language of great simplicity to speak to God (Abba, Father), a language full of surprises and daring images to speak to each other so as to echo what God has said (Bible and doctrine). Jesus in his ministry, his death, and his resurrection creates a human group where it ought to be hard to make "easy speeches."

The reference to what writers say about the process of writing reminds us that every search for truth involves some kind of "fleeing," some kind of asceticism. Every act of imaginative creation, in science as well as art, needs silence, a wariness about what looks easy. And at a time when politics is increasingly dominated by people's worries about appearance and presentation, about "how it will play"; when the culture of celebrity is a daily trading in illusory images; when show business reaches out tentacles in all directions, we need to know when and how to flee. And we need to bear in mind that it is not other people's folly we are running from so much as our own deep-rooted propensity to be drawn into these games. Remember Macarius's blunt summary, that the world is a place where they make you do stupid things.

II.

One implication of this need to flee is a possible new definition of at least part of what's involved in being a person of faith today (or in any age, really): being a believer is manifest in how we talk, in what we think of language. What if you could recognize people of faith by how they spoke? By an absence of cliché or of dehumanizing mockery or glib consolations? And what if conversion meant taking on not just a new vocabulary and new ideas but a new style of talking? The "world" is a place where it is barely possible to speak without making things more difficult and destructive. The commonwealth of God is a place where speech is restored, in praise, in patience, in *attentive* speaking (which is bound up with attentive listening). This is not about any kind of despairing silence, being silent because there is nothing to say or know or because you're always going to be misunderstood. It is more of an *expectant* quiet, the quiet before the dawn, when you don't want to say anything too quickly for fear of spoiling what's uncovered for you as the light comes.

Thomas Merton (one of the many who have written about the desert fathers and mothers in recent times) was exercising a very Christian and very monastic vocation when he wrote his essays in the sixties about the strange things that happened to language when it was used for advertising and propaganda.[16] Monastic life above all has to be a life in which what is said is integrally part of a style and rhythm of living, a life in which silence is natural, expectant, and bound up with a right and creative kind of speaking to God and each other.

Some writers of the last few decades (including Merton himself) have spoken of the way in which any and all of us can "internalize" monasticism and live the contemplative dimension of life in the midst of an active world. Perhaps one of the best ways to do this is to learn how to x-ray our talking. It sounds frightening, because we think it suggests a severe and condemnatory atmosphere where we are always liable to be reported to the thought police for idle words. But the truth is that we are looking or listening here for speech that will affirm and open the way to life, for a speech that can be playful and not just useful, for words that disturb and change us not because they threaten but because they "fit" a reality we are just beginning to discern. If communities of faith took language this seriously, they would be extraordinary signs of transformation. And while the desert tradition has nothing much to say about this directly, we ought to be thinking about some of this as we search for new words, songs, and prayers for our worship; how easily this too becomes a sphere where easy speeches take over, where our words say too little or try to say too much in the wrong key, where we end up sounding flat or pompous or both. But that is a long story, and not one with a short resolution.

The language of worship reminds us of one theological reason why language matters to Christians. In worship, we try to "put ourselves under the Word of God," as the saying is; we try to bring our minds and hearts into harmony with what God has said and is saying, in Jesus and in the words of Scripture. We remember that God made all things by an act of self-communication, and when we respond to his speaking, we are searching for some way of reflecting, echoing that self-communication. But the same is true in all of our relationships, not just in what happens in worship. If God has made all things by the Word, then each person and thing exists because God *is speaking* to it and in it. If we are to respond adequately, truthfully, we must listen for the word God speaks to and through each element of the creation—hence the importance of listening in expectant silence.

To borrow an image that appears in some of the ancient Hindu texts, we might think of the creative Word as spoken into the vast cavern of potential that is the first moment of created existence; from that darkness come countless echoes of the first eternal Word, the "harmonics" hidden in that primal sound. When we rightly respond to, relate to, anyone or anything, it is as if we have found the note to sing that is in harmony with the creating Word. Or, to use language more familiar in Eastern Christian thinking, each living being in the world rests upon a unique creative act of God, a unique communication from God within the infinite self-communication that is the one eternal Word. Every being has at its heart its own word, its own "logos."[17] A truthful relation to anything is an uncovering of that word.

In a recent book on the use of music therapy with autistic children, there is a memorable description of how the therapist has to listen and react.[18] You let the child make what noise it wants to with the instruments put out on the floor, and you listen with all your attention until some kind of pattern or rhythm begins to emerge. When it does, you gradually begin to make some kind of pattern of noise yourself that echoes what the child is producing; communication begins, and something emerges that was not there before. So also with our cooperation with and response to the Word of God: an intensive listening for the rhythm of divine life in what may at first seem to be unintelligible, and a gradual learning of how to echo it, to make sounds in union with it.

Christians talk about "speaking the truth in love" quite a bit, but in this context, this doesn't mean charitably telling other people exactly where they've gone wrong. It means finding a way to speak to them that resonates with the creative word working in their depths. Love is not a feeling of goodwill toward the neighbor but the active search for that word—so that I can hear what God has to say to me and give to me through the neighbor, and also so that I can speak to what is real in the neighbor, not what suits or interests me and my agenda. Sometimes this means that what at first looks like the "loving" response won't quite do—and the desert literature shows some keen awareness of this at times.[19] A certain degree of hesitation in our willingness to offer the first kind of help that comes to our minds is no bad thing if it means that we end up attending to the reality of someone else, rather than to the pressure that comes from wanting to make *myself* feel better. And that word *hesitation* is one that the French philosopher Simone Weil put at the center of her vision of how we should relate to each other in love:[20] we "hesitate" as we might do on the threshold of some new territory, some unexplored interior. It is an aspect of our reverence for each other, and I think that it is an effective modern translation of quite a lot of what the desert fathers and mothers meant by "fleeing."

All this should make us think a bit harder about how we as Christians approach ethics. It is quite clearly no part of the intention of the desert teachers to promote anything like "situation ethics"—just think what the most loving thing would be and do that. That would be to give way to the silliest kind of "listening to the heart" and to invite endless delusion and disaster. But if the desert literature is right, then we all need training in listening and attending almost more than anything else. Unless we are capable of patience before each other, before the mysteriousness of each other, it's very unlikely that we will do God's will with any kind of fullness. Without a basic education in attention, no deeply ethical behavior is really going to be possible. We may keep the rules and do what is technically and externally the right thing, But that "doing the right" will not be grounded yet in who we are, in the *person* God wants us to become, and it may not survive stress and temptation. It may also be quite capable of existing alongside attitudes and habits dangerous to ourselves and each other; it may not bring us life with and through the neighbor. Our Christian codes of behavior quite rightly tell us that some sorts of action are always wrong—torture or fraud, killing the innocent or the unborn, sexual violence and infidelity—but to see why that is so requires us to go back a step or two to see why this or that action is bound to speak of inattention, why this or that action makes it impossible to listen for the word in another person. Unless we can grasp something of that, our ethics will never really be integrated with our search and our prayer for holy life in community.

Christian ethics in fact is poised between two different sorts of consideration that are not easy to hold together in theory. The first is a strong and uncompromising conviction of what sorts of behavior appropriately honor God, especially God's image in human beings and God's purpose in the material creation. And second, an equally strong suspicion of the kind of instruction and exhortation that gives one person or set of persons control over others in a way that damages everyone. The desert literature does not offer any theoretical solution to this. Rather, it presents stories of people learning from each other. "Do

what you see me doing" says the elder to the novice asking for guidance;[21] in other words, watch patiently how a
Christian behaves. And this is not a claim by the elder
to have arrived at perfection (any more than this is true
of Paul's plea to his converts to be imitators of him as he
is of Christ in 1 Cor. 11:1). What the novice must witness
is also the daily acknowledgment of failure and exposure
to judgment, the daily loving *withdrawal* from a position of
safe and authoritative superiority. This is what has to be
learned, and perhaps it becomes a paradox when written
down, since most of us know that the impulse to change
our life commonly arises when someone is not ordering
us to do so but is presenting to us, as a gift, the possibility
of living otherwise. Remember again that the holy person
is the one who does *not* make you think first of all, "That
looks really hard."

Our Christian speaking, then, arises out of "fleeing,"
running from what makes us feel smug and in control,
what gratifies our longing for approval and respect. In silence, as Abba Bessarion observes, you have no chance to
compare yourself with others[22]—and we have seen how
the tradition discourages any kind of comparison, with
even the great Anthony being brought down to earth by
discovering who his equal in the spirit is. It is not that
talking is evil or that it necessarily cheapens the truth.
After all, if God himself communicates and does so in
human terms, in the life and speech of Jesus, in the witness

of Scripture, there must be talking that is wonderful, rev-
elatory, transfiguring, that takes us into the heart of things.
When we have found the word or phrase that anchors us
in prayer, the mantra that stills and focuses us, we are discovering something of the grace and power of real language that attunes us to God's communication in a
relation that is somehow both speaking and silence. It is
simply that for most of the time we do not take language
seriously enough. We haven't understood Jesus's warning
that we will be called to account for every word we waste
(Matt. 12:36)—which presumably means every word that
does not in some way contribute to the building up of
myself and my neighbor as persons maturing in the life of
grace. Nonwasted words may be serious or playful (we
misunderstand this if we think Jesus is just telling us to be
austere and businesslike in what we say), but they are all
words in tune with the word God speaks in creating—
which is why art and beauty and even certain sorts of
humor are not alien to the work of grace. The times when
we can be absolutely sure that we are wasting words are
when we are reinforcing our reputation, defending our
position at someone else's expense—looking for a standard of comparison, a currency in the market of virtue.

And nonwasted words take time to mature; they must
come from depth, and so from the quiet and expectancy
already described. At first we won't find truthful and creative words coming easily. Only those who have matured

some in the contemplative dimension of life with God can give the impression of speaking, not easily in the sense of glibly, but out of an inner world in which they are at home without self-consciousness. The rest of us need to put some hard work into monitoring our talk. "Just listen to yourself!" we sometimes say to a person when we want to correct his or her careless or offensive talk; it is excellent advice for all seasons. Language is not an evil, but the way we so often use it means that a lot is lost when we start talking. Here is one of the most eloquent desert stories about this:

> They said about Abba Apollo that he had a disciple called Isaac who was fully trained in all sorts of good actions. He had the gift of uninterrupted prayer during the celebration of the Eucharist. When he came to church, he did not let anyone join him—he would say that everything is good in its own time, but there is a right time for everything. As soon as the liturgy was over, he would flee as if he were running from a fire and hurry back to his cell. At the end of the Eucharist, it is common practice for the brothers to be given a piece of bread and a cup of wine, but this man would not receive these. It was not that he wanted to turn his back on the love feast of

the brethren, but he wanted to preserve the uninterrupted prayer he had been experiencing during the celebration of the Sacrament.

It so happened that he fell ill; the brothers heard about this and came to visit him, and while they were sitting with him, they asked, "Abba, why do you flee from the brethren at the end of the liturgy?" He said to them, "I am not running away from the brethren but from the evil tricks of the demons. If you hang around in the open air when you're holding a lighted lamp, the wind will make the lamp go out. We are just the same. If we hang around away from our cells when we are illuminated by the Holy Spirit, our spirit goes dark."[23]

It is worth recalling this when we think how deeply we prize the visible signs of fellowship that follow most acts of worship. The love feast is a great good—Isaac doesn't dispute the value of the coffee and cookies. But something very distinctive has happened when it feels difficult to break the silence, when we are afraid of letting the lamp be blown out. Even in the secular environment, we recognize this at times. In the film *Shakespeare in Love*, the end of the first performance of *Romeo and Juliet* is greeted initially with a stunned silence—you can see the actors briefly wondering whether it has been a total failure, but what has happened is that the audience has been taken out of the "easy" world into another level of language and experience. The applause takes time to come, but when it does, it is overwhelming. And the moment of quiet at the end of a play or concert that has moved us deeply is something we all know. Like Isaac, we may well want to run to our cells rather than break the moment with talk. The time may come, but it will have taken time to reach the point where words become possible. Even Isaac finds words, memorable words, when he is challenged.

Keeping the light steady, taking the time needed for real speech to emerge, withdrawing from the easy reaction, the obvious phrase, the habitual and stale mode of speaking and acting—all this implies very clearly the need for stability, for an environment where you can indeed take the time that is needed. Fleeing is not about constant relocation. There is all the difference in the world between running from responsibility and "fleeing" for the sake of truth or honesty—that is, for the sake of responsibility. The desert tradition has a great deal to say about the temptation to think that going somewhere else will make things easier. The truth is that running and staying put are two sides of the same coin in the desert literature. Both are about finding the way to avoid the compulsive following of your individual (not personal) agenda. What you are ultimately "running" from is your compulsions, and in the desert fathers' sense, in "fleeing" you are making a break for freedom. So it isn't a matter of trying to run away from yourself but running away *to* yourself, to the identity you are not allowed to recognize or nurture or grow so long as you are stuck in the habits of anxious comparison, status seeking, and chatter. As so often in these considerations, we have to think about this as a discovery of space, room to breathe. The work of living and dying with the neighbor has to do with giving someone else the room to find his or her connection with God. And the acceptance of different callings in the name of a truly personal community has to do with making sure that your development of your own vocation isn't squeezing out someone else's. And the call to flee from privilege, safety, speech (and bishops), is a call to put some distance between yourself and the less than personal pressures of soul, temptations that stunt your growth, which the Greek Christian tradition calls *pathe*, "passions"—or pressures on the soul to pull it out of its centeredness in God.

The desert fathers and mothers speak of a life in which there is space, and they are committed to finding that space of divine opportunity within very limited territory. The desert may look big in the photographs, but the desert as experienced is also the size of your own heart and mind and imagination, and these are not infinite spaces. Indeed, they may be very restricted ones. And the commitment to stay within the "space" of these particular people's company, these daily disciplines, this unchanging environment, material and mental, is costly. It takes time to discover that the apparently generous horizon of a world in which our surface desires have free play is in fact a tighter prison than the constrained space chosen by the desert ascetics. When we have learned more or less successfully to "flee" some of the illusory landscapes in which life appears easier, we still have to learn how to inhabit the landscape of truth as more than an occasional visitor.

4.

STAYING

I.

We do not know a great deal about the desert mothers. There are a number of names that survive, such as Amma Syncletica's. The women seem to have lived in communities of their own. There is not much suggestion in the sayings that survive that they were exclusively under the direction of the men. Indeed, this is a mixed blessing from an historical perspective. Because of the strong insistence for men and women in this period to be separate, it would have been unusual for a male ascetic to be directing female ascetics in the desert. Some mothers, like Amma Syncletica, are very independent figures, women of real spiritual weight and authority. At the beginning of the fourth century, Saint Methodius, who taught in Asia Minor, wrote a dialogue set in a community of women. In this dialogue female figures are given the role of expounding on aspects of the spiritual life and the Bible. Although written by a man, it shows that women could be expected to know about such things and be listened to as teachers.

A second example is from later in the fourth century in the person of Saint Macrina, the sister of the two great Cappadocian theologians Basil and Gregory. Gregory wrote a life of his sister. A dialogue he also wrote on the soul of the resurrection depicts him visiting Macrina on her deathbed, from which they have a dialogue about the nature of the soul and the nature of desire. It is a fascinating dialogue in itself, but what is notable is that throughout, Gregory refers to Macrina as "the teacher." So it is not entirely a man's world in the fourth century, even in the desert.

Although the mothers of the desert have been mentioned often enough in these pages, their recorded sayings amount to a very small percentage of the total. They were still women in a man's world, for all that they are regarded with equal respect as far as their actual teaching goes. But perhaps it is appropriate to turn to one of them—Amma Syncletica—at this point for an image that some might think characteristically feminine:

> If you are living in a monastic community, do
> not go to another place: it will do you a great
> deal of harm. If a bird abandons the eggs she
> has been sitting on, she prevents them from
> hatching, and in the same way monks or nuns
> will grow cold and their faith will perish if
> they go around from one place to another.[1]

The theme is a very frequent one—suggesting that this was one of the commonest problems in the desert. A saying of Abba Moses is probably the most often quoted on this question: "Sit in your cell and your cell will teach you everything."[2] Learning to stay where you are becomes one of the hardest lessons of the desert, harder than apparently tougher forms of asceticism. Bearing your own company and the company of those immediately and unavoidably around you requires some very special graces, as John the Dwarf insists:

> If a man has the tools God gives, he will be
> able to stay in his cell, even if he has none of
> the tools of this world. And if he has the tools
> of this world but lacks the tools God gives, he
> can still use those tools to stay in his cell. But if
> he has neither God's tools nor those of this
> world, it is completely impossible for him to
> stay in the cell.[3]

We can cope with a certain level of demand for stability if we have some of the resources provided by the world, some of the skills that monastic life tries to strip us of. But precisely because monastic life, the contemplative dimension of life, seeks to take away our capacity to distract ourselves in the usual way, by self-dramatizing and fantasy,[4] we have a real problem if we are not open to

God's grace. The problem is not just simple boredom; it is what the Greek tradition refers to as *akedia*, one of the eight great pressures on the soul identified by the expert diagnosticians of the fifth century and later. It has to do with frustration, helplessness, lack of motivation, the displacement of stresses and difficulties from the inner to the outer world. It is described classically by Evagrius and Cassian in their writings on the "passions."

The morning is wearing on, getting hotter and stickier; there is still a long time to go before eating or any other break in the routine. Hours spent plaiting reeds for making baskets have left you feeling numb and bored. Is there any progress at all to be seen? Or is this life as featureless as the sand around? Surely making progress would be more possible elsewhere; after all, in this dead landscape, you have no chance to share what you discover, even if you do finally manage to discover something. And then, this must be a selfish life: surely there's one of the brothers who'd like a visit, who needs something? And wouldn't life be more useful in the city, anyway? That's where the real need is, and where one could truly be effective. Anywhere but here, anywhere but now.

You don't have to be a hermit to appreciate this; anyone who lives with a routine will recognize the symptoms instantly.

It strikes us most often in the form of that deep anxiety of whether, as Evagrius said, we are really serving

God. Or the feeling "Is this what it was all for?" I have
signed the fifteenth letter of the morning and made the
fourth uncomfortable phone call. I have emerged from a
meeting about next year's budget, and I am getting ready
for a session with our investment advisors after lunch.
After which I have to go and take an afternoon's school
assembly. Probably in the evening, I'll have to institute a
new parish priest somewhere. All of it is all right. All of it
has also got to be done. But I think, "Was it all for this?"
The only thing I find that helps is to let myself be simply
drawn into the present moment. This means making a
point sometimes of looking at what is on this side of the
window pane in the office or putting my hands on the
arms of a chair and feeling the fabric. And breathing, saying, "Well, here I am. This is what I must do next; the bas-
ket-weaving stuff." And, well, who knows whether this is
the service of God? All I can do here and now is to say,
"God is in this moment."

In John, chapter 12, Jesus says, "Where I am, there will
my servant be." Well, then where the servant is, there also
Christ is. How do you learn to be with Christ at the
Diocesan Board of Finance? How do you learn to be with
Christ when you are dealing with a clerical marriage in
difficulties? How do you learn to be with Christ when
you are counting to twenty over an irritating letter of
angry complaint that you have just received about something you have no particular responsibility for? You have

to be with Christ there, because Christ is with you there. "Where I am in glory, there will my servant be." To open that moment to God just by letting myself be drawn into the present moment—that's my cure for akedia.

The fact is that none of us wants to start where we are: the legendary response to the inquiry about how to get to wherever-it-is, "I wouldn't start from here," is exactly what we are feeling. And if, in the context of the desert and its practices and disciplines, we have in some sense been brought to where we really are, acquainted with who we really are, it is worse, not better. The distractions are not there, the games we can play in our relations with others for psychic exercise and reassurance are forbidden (if we have been paying any attention to our spiritual guides). The ego flounders, whines, postures, and pleads, and the obvious, the compelling, the practically unanswerable solution to it all is after all within our power. Change what we can: move.

Evagrius knew about it, as did all the Eastern monastic fathers. Saint Benedict, too, wrote acidly about "gyrovagues, monks who are constantly on the road looking for a community to suit them: anywhere but here, any colleagues but these."[4] One of the anonymous sayings also notes how we can deceive ourselves when we travel around looking for a spiritual guide who really suits us: the old man in this anecdote asks the young seeker whether he is actually looking not for an elder who can tell him what to do but for one who does what he—the "customer"—wants: "Is that what you are after to bring you peace?"[5]

We are easily persuaded that the problem of growing up in the life of the spirit can be located outside ourselves. Somewhere else I could be nicer, holier, more balanced, more detached about criticism, more disciplined, able to sing in tune, and probably thinner as well. Somewhere there is a saintly person who really understands me (and so won't make life difficult for me). Unreality has a huge advantage over reality in some ways, since it is not obliged to obey any laws of cause and effect. But there's the catch—you are involved in those laws. So:

> If a trial comes upon you in the place where
> you live, do not leave that place when the trial
> comes. Wherever you go, you will find that
> what you are running from is there ahead of
> you. So stay until the trial is over, so that if you
> do end up leaving, no offense will be caused,
> and you will not bring distress to others who
> live in the same neighborhood.[6]

It is a very typical consideration that you should not be quick to move, because of the message you will send to anyone in the same situation. ("Don't bother; it can't be done here, with these people.") The inescapable itch and

ache of living with yourself is even more vividly brought
out in one of the anonymous stories:

> There was once a brother in a monastery who
> had a rather turbulent temperament; he often
> became angry. So he said to himself, "I will go
> and live on my own. If I have nothing to do
> with anyone else, I will live in peace and my
> passions will be soothed." Off he went to live
> in solitude in a cave. One day when he had
> filled his jug with water, he put it on the
> ground and it tipped over. So he picked it up
> and filled it again—and again it tipped over.
> He filled it a third time, put it down, and over
> it went again. He was furious: he grabbed the
> jug and smashed it. And then came to his senses
> and realized that he had been tricked by the
> devil. He said, "Since I have been defeated, even
> in solitude, I'd better go back to the monastery.
> Conflict is to be met everywhere, but so is pa-
> tience and so is the help of God." So he got
> up and went back where he came from.[7]

If you find relationships difficult, what will you do
about your relationship with yourself, your own body,
the cussedness of ordinary things? Sin and struggle are
not just about what you do to others. Conflict is to be

met everywhere, not least in facing ourselves. So to stay in the cell is most fundamentally to stay in touch with the reality of who I am as a limited creature, as someone who is not in control of everything, whether inner or outer, as an unfinished being in the hands of the maker. The brother in the story has achieved an impressive level of "spiritual" attainment but is no less an unfinished person. What he has to learn is that his real spiritual maturity still needs the time it will take for his whole personal life to be pervaded by God and for the passions, the pressures on the soul, otherwise known as temptations, to be dealt with.

So there is a relentlessly prosaic element in the journey to holiness. Never mind the ecstasies and the feats of self-denial, never mind the heroics: the essential task is whatever is there to be done next.

> A brother asked one of the old men: "What shall I do? I'm obsessed by this nagging thought, 'You can't fast and you can't work, so at least go and visit the sick, because that's a loving thing to do.'" The old man recognized that the devil had been sowing his seeds and said to him, "Go. Eat, drink, sleep, just don't leave your cell." He was well aware that it is endurance in the cell that makes a monk what he ought to be.

For three days the brother did just this, and
then he was overcome with *akedia* [spiritual
lassitude and apathy]. But he found some little
palm leaves and started trimming them. Next
day he started plaiting them; when he felt
hungry, he said, "Here are some more palm
leaves; I'll prepare them, and then have something to eat." He finished them and said, "Perhaps I'll read for a little bit before eating."
When he had done some reading, he said,
"Now let's sing a few psalms and then I can
eat with a good conscience."

And so by God's help he went on little by
little, until he had indeed become what he was
meant to become.[8]

Examples could be multiplied of this almost painfully
undramatic account of what you have to do to be holy. We
want something very tangible, something substantial to
mark the difference that has been made in our lives, and
we are recommended simply to get on with it, whatever
humdrum matter "it" is. We are even warned, in this little
anecdote, to beware of looking eagerly for someone to
love—using someone else to solve the problem of our
boredom and our fear of ourselves. It should probably be
said that practically all the desert elders are utterly clear
that when a specific human need presents itself, we should

respond. The point is not some abstract doctrine of the superiority of solitude to active charity but simply that the anxious search for an object of charity is about us rather than about the concrete call to love the neighbor.

Yet again, Annie Dillard comes to mind, describing the ways in which we avoid getting down to the actual time-taking work of doing what needs doing (we want to have done it). And she writes that "appealing workplaces are to be avoided. One wants a room with no view, so imagination can meet memory in the dark."[9] The staying in the cell of the desert is likewise a "room with no view" in this sense, a place where the self can encounter itself. The anguish of starting when we long to have done it already, the anguish of confronting an inner landscape in which, when you look honestly, there seems no hope of getting it in order, is vividly conveyed in another of the anonymous stories:

> A brother fell when he was tempted, and in his distress he stopped practicing his monastic rule. He really longed to take it up again, but his own misery prevented him. He would say to himself, "When shall I be able to be holy in the way I used to be before?"
>
> He went to see one of the old men and told him all about himself. And when the old man learned of his distress, he said: "There was a

man who had a plot of land, but it got neg-
lected and turned into waste ground, full of
weeds and brambles. So he said to his son, 'Go
and weed the ground.' The son went off to
weed it, saw all the brambles, and despaired.
He said to himself, 'How long will it take before I have uprooted and reclaimed all of that?'
So he lay down and went to sleep for several
days. His father came to see how he was getting on and found he had done nothing at all.
'Why have you done nothing?' he said. The
son replied, 'Father, when I started to look at
this and saw how many weeds and brambles
there were, I was so depressed that I could do
nothing but lie down on the ground.' His father said, 'Child, just go over the surface of the
plot every day and you will make some
progress.' So he did, and before long the whole
plot was weeded. The same is true for you,
brother: work just a little bit without getting
discouraged, and God by his grace will
reestablish you." [10]

Reluctant gardeners will know the feeling exactly.
But most of us can identify with the impulse to go to
sleep for several days when faced with the sense of what
needs changing in our lives. The desert elders would have

understood very well the child's riddle about how you eat an elephant (a bit at a time). And the whole of their understanding of human growth and human healing assumes that trying not to go to sleep for several days, trying not to act as if the problem of myself will just go away or solve itself or get solved by a new environment, is the toughest challenge of "spirituality," one that not every self-help book on spiritual growth will give you honest guidance about. The guidance we need is not so much how not to be bored but how to face boredom without terror, not so much how to greet everything with spiritual joy and excitement but how to preserve the quite motivation to keep our eyes open.

One of the essential teachings I have taken from John Main and the Christian contemplative tradition that he represents is the importance of a particular kind of stability or faithfulness in the daily practice of meditation. In being faithful to and with the mantra we are *staying*. That relates directly to what the desert fathers teach about stability. The whole practice of staying with the mantra and the discipline of meditating, the saying of the prayer "formula," makes most sense within the context of the kind of life the desert fathers talk about. That means a life where we are always trying to put our self-preoccupation and self-dramatizing, our compulsion to be in charge to one side.

But more specifically, the very notion of praying—

meditating in this form of Christian meditation as taught by John Main—stems from the desert tradition. John Cassian, who was so important to John Main, was a monk who flourished in the fourth century and made it his life's work to explore, digest, and summarize the teachings of the great desert fathers. Cassian's work consists of the Conferences, as they are called, which are of a series of interviews with the great old men. Cassian and his friends went around to their huts and caves in the desert saying, "Would you like to tell us your views on this and that, Father?" and scribbling down their replies. From that the whole notion of prayer oriented around the repeated "formula," as Cassian in Latin calls the mantra, first arises. In the literature from the Syrian desert of the same period come the first examples of the Jesus Prayer—contemplative prayer using the rhythmic repetition of "Lord Jesus Christ, Son of God, have mercy on me a sinner"—in its various forms. This is also the form of prayer used with the Eastern rosary. As it is from this world that these important traditions of contemplative prayer come, it does help people today who are seeking to meditate to understand something about that world and how these practices of prayer fitted into it.

II.

One of the most telling images for the importance of staying is in the advice given by another nameless elder to a brother struggling with temptation: "Go. Sit in your cell and give your body in pledge to the walls."[11] You have to *promise* yourself to yourself and to your actual environment, as if you were settling a proposal of marriage. You have to "espouse" reality rather than unreality, the actual limits of where and who you are rather than the world of magic in which anything can happen if you want it to. The fantasy world is one in which I am not promised, espoused, to my body and my history—with all that this entails about my family, my work, my literal physical surroundings, the people I must live with, the language I must speak, and so on. It is a rather startling intensification of the command to love yourself in the right way. Sometimes, when Christian writers have tried to explain what it meant for Satan to revolt against God and fall from heaven, they have suggested that Satan preferred the idea of an unreal world of which he was in charge to a real world in which all glory was due to God. It is not a bad definition of the essence of evil. And it means that there is no goodness that is not bodily and realistic and local.

Perhaps this is the key to understanding the temptation of Jesus to worship Satan in exchange for "all the kingdoms of the world"? It's not as though Satan owns the kingdoms of the real world so as to be able to dispose of them. All the temptations of Jesus seem to be about resorting to magic instead of working with the fabric of the real world. Jesus performs miracles in his ministry, of course, but never as a substitute for the hard material work of changing how people see God and never as a substitute for the bodily cost of love, which reaches its climax on the cross. Satan wants Jesus to join him in the world where cause and effect don't matter, the world of magic. And Jesus refuses, determined to stay in the desert with its hunger and boredom, to stay in the human world with its conflict and risk. He refuses to compel and manipulate people into faith, because it can only be the act of a person, and persons do not live in the magic world.

Indeed, we could well say that Jesus above all is literally "a body pledged to the walls," to the limits of this world. His Body the church is "promised" to the end of time, never defeated by Satan's forces, and that means that in this body Jesus works with all the limitations, the fragility, and the folly of the human beings he summons to be with him. He does not stop working in the church when we Christians are wicked and stupid and lazy. The church is not magic, much as we should love it to be—a realm where problems are solved instantly and special revelations answer all our questions and provide a shortcut through all our conflicts. It is preeminently and crucially a community of persons in the sense that we have already explored, and so it is a place where holiness takes time and where the prose of daily faithfulness and, yes, sometimes daily boredom have to be faced and blessed, not shunned or concealed. And in the sacrament of the Eucharist, we see in visible and tangible form what it means for Jesus to be pledged to this world, the Body that is always there as the community gives thanks with him and through him. Those Christian traditions accustomed to reserve the bread and wine of the Sacrament and to give veneration to places where the sacrament is kept will have some particularly strong associations with this idea. Some Catholic devotional manuals of an earlier generation used to speak of Christ in the reserved Sacrament as the "Prisoner of Love," and although some now find this awkward or sentimental language, it expresses something quite central to the belief in Jesus's fidelity to the world he comes to transform. But it was the Protestant philosopher Kierkegaard who put it most uncompromisingly when he said that once Jesus had accepted the human form, it was as if he could not have taken it off even if he had wanted to.[12] It's an absurd way of talking, as Kierkegaard acknowledges, but again it crystallizes something central and makes us think again about what we do when we speak of Jesus as equally present in his Body and as the "spouse" of the church, his pledged bride.

The church needs to see itself as essentially a place where "pledging" is visible, if it is a community where Jesus's characteristic way of working is shared and shown forth. It exists in an environment in which this talk of pledging the body will sound very eccentric indeed. We are, most of us in the Western world, more physically mobile than ever. We expect change and variety in our work. We have less and less interest in or commitment as a society to the ideal of sexual faithfulness. We are entertained by deliberately hectic and rapid images. It isn't difficult in this world to start imagining that the body is really a sort of tool for the will to use in getting its entertainment and satisfaction, its sense of power and fulfillment. Occasionally we are brought up short: physical illness or disability doesn't fit well with this picture; neither does really intense and selfless love. Even bad weather makes us think twice about how confidently we can say we're in charge of the environment. But the pressures (the passions) are there in great strength, and we need disciplines to remind ourselves and each other of why the "pledged" body is such an essential notion for human growing.

The church celebrates fidelity. It blesses marriage, the most obvious sign of the pledging of bodies. But it also blesses the vows of monastic life and solitary life equally as signs of promise and fidelity. It lives by the regular round of worship, the daily prayer of believers, the constant celebration of the Eucharist, meeting the same potentially difficult or dull people time after time, because they are the soil of growth. It insists that we go on reading the same book and reciting the same creeds, not so as to limit and control, but to make sure that we promise to go on listening to what we believe is an inexhaustible story, a pattern of words and images given by God that we will never come to the end of. And quite concretely too, there is the way in which a Christian church can be a sign of fidelity, of a pledged body, in a community from which so much has fled or drained away: communities of poverty or drabness, without much to show in the way of religion or morals or culture to interest the person looking for stimulus. In very unmagical settings indeed, inner cities and prisons, remote hamlets and struggling mission stations, the church remains pledged: its pastors and people and buildings speaking of a God who is not bored or disillusioned by what he has made. And so they speak of the personal possibilities for everyone in such a situation.

The church is always renewed from the edges rather than from the center. There is a limit to what the institutional church can do. Institutions have their own dynamic and their own problems, and renewal tends not to come from central planning. It was Saint Francis who went to Pope Innocent III, not the other way around. And nobody planned the role that Benedictinism was going to have in the church's history and in Europe's history or its role in teaching meditation today.

The parish structure works up to a point. It is one among a number of ways of being church. For many people, in addition to parochial loyalties, there are cross-parochial loyalties and networks that feed and sustain them, like The World Community for Christian Meditation. What needs to happen within the parish structure, as well as what happens among networks across these very good structures, is a re-visioning. Nearly all Christians have inherited a functional idea of what local Christian community is for. It is there to gather us for the sacraments. I think we need to break the hold of that functionalism. We need to recognize that in addition to the sacraments, we meet for another kind of togetherness in parish life, in study and prayer. This means challenging the dominance of the Sunday-based model.

As time passes it will be harder to think that the future of the church will take one clear and uniform institutional shape across the globe or even through local communities. In some areas, the church is already beginning to exist in parallel lines, not in sealed compartments but in different styles and idioms and with real interchange. The challenge lies in the discovery of a church renewed in contemplation, across the cultural frontiers of our world.

Another question those of us who have the freedom to do so need to go on asking is where the unity of the church lies. Or in what that unity consists. I believe it is a unity that fundamentally exists in the shared gaze toward Christ, and through Christ to the Father. If we believe that our unity comes from that looking together into a mystery and occasionally nudging one another and saying, "Look at that!" it can help us to feel how the unity we enjoy is not primarily about institutional uniformity, saying the same words all the time. The unity is found in the common direction we are looking. But we must be willing to nudge one another and describe what we are seeing—whether in or out of the parish. Unfolding that dimension of unity is one way to make more space within the church for the contemplative dimension. If not enough people are looking into the mystery, unity comes to be seen in merely functionalist terms. We meet for events. We discharge our obligations. We sign up and do our duties. But we miss the vital and living element of unity.

In short, a church that is faithful to its basic task is telling people that willingness to be who they are, and to begin to change only from the point of that recognition, is fundamental in the encounter with God. People can imagine that religious faith represents a deep restlessness, a dissatisfaction with the ordinary and the material, that it is poetry, not prose. They are not wrong about the poetry. But poetry has to be made out of profoundly ordinary experience, in the words that everyone uses. Practically all the great religious traditions insist at some point that holiness involves a new encounter with the prosaic along the way to transformation. And Christianity, as I have been suggesting, has a particular theological reason for valuing the local and material: God has acted and spoken directly in the material of a human life, in the language of ordinary vulnerability. The divinity of Christ is not some "internal" fact about him; it is what his entire human existence, soul and body, makes present (which is why in

the early church, it mattered so much not to identify the
divinity of Jesus with his mind or spirit but to see it as per-
vading his entire identity).

That the church will not fail is one promise we can
trust. This is for the simple reason that the church is above
all the community of those whom Jesus calls to receive
the Spirit and to share the relation that he has to his Father, his source. Because Jesus does not stop issuing that
invitation, the church does not stop existing.

III.

Christianity encourages me to be faithful to the body that
I am—a body that can be hurt, a body that is always living
in the middle of limitations; it encourages me to accept
unavoidable frustration in this material and accident-
prone existence without anger. To talk about pledging the
body to the walls in the sense of the fundamental decision
to be where and who I am is also to open the door to the
recognition carried in another of the sayings of Amma
Syncletica:

> There are many who live in the mountains
> and behave as if they were in the towns. You
> can be a solitary in your mind even when you
> live in the middle of a crowd. And you can be
> a solitary and still live in the middle of the
> crowd of your own thoughts.[13]

When external solitude is accompanied by the jostling crowd of fantasies and longings and fugues of speculation, the body is not really pledged to that solitude. But the body itself can be a hermitage when I have embraced it as quite simply the place where I know I will meet God—the here and now of my actual humanity. And solitude becomes possible, the kind of solitude that is expressed in the "death to the neighbor," the lack of judgment, the reticence in speech that we have observed in the desert. Grace returns us to the particular and local. Just as there are no neighbors in the abstract (neighbors we want to go and look for to satisfy our own desire to be useful), only the actual human material around us, so there is no individual soul in the abstract, only the human material of my body, my words, my memories; my gifts, my weaknesses. The lawyer in the gospel who asked, "Who is my neighbor?" and prompted the parable of the Good Samaritan (Luke 15: 11–32) was asking a perfectly serious question at one level, because the command to love the neighbor isn't abstract; the pity was that he needed to be shown what was under his nose. Like most of us.

Only the body saves the soul. It sounds rather shocking put like that, but the point is that the soul left to itself, the inner life or whatever you want to call it, is not capable of transforming itself. It needs the gifts that only the external life can deliver: the actual events of God's action in history, heard by physical ears; the actual material fact of the meeting of believers where bread and wine are shared; the actual wonderful, disagreeable, impossible, unpredictable human beings we encounter daily, in and out of the church. Only in this setting do we become holy, and holy in a way unique to each one of us.

It has been said that sanctity is inimitable. While I can think of some very holy people who cry out for imitation because of all their quirks of behavior, the imitability in question is not of that kind. I cannot become holy by copying another's path. Like the novice in the desert, I must watch the elders and learn the shape and the rhythm of being Christian from those who have walked further and worked harder. And then I have to take my own steps and create a life that has never been lived before. At the day of Judgment, as we are often reminded, the question will not be about why we failed to be someone else. I will not be asked why I wasn't Martin Luther King or Mother Teresa but why I wasn't Rowan Williams. The journey is always one that leads into more, not less, uniqueness. It's all to do once again with the call to be persons, not individuals.

The desert looks shapeless—the sandy desert of Egypt especially, where the sand shifts and landscapes dissolve. It looks like nowhere in particular. Yet you go into it so as to become more particular than ever. In the modern context, you could compare it with the other sort of nonplace we are familiar with: places stripped of any local identity, featureless and totally unsurprising—the airport lounge, the fast-food outlet, places designed entirely for individuals looking for repeatable experiences. No doubt fourth-century Alexandria had its equivalents: our job, as particular people trying to live something of a calling to contemplation, as a *church* looking for renewal and integrity, is to seek out the nonplaces where we can become personally faithful. We need to identify those bits of our immediate environment that can serve as sites for recovering a covenant with the self and the body. Like Annie Dillard writing about writing, we have to find somewhere dark enough for memory and imagination to join hands. Not harsh places whose austerity is itself distracting, not comfortable ones where we can drift away from the here and now, but simply places to settle and make friends with ourselves before God. This is as much true for our daily prayers as for retreats or longer-term commitments. You can, as Amma Syncletica says, be alone anywhere, but learning that may need some very well-thought-out strategies along the way.

So we come back to the beginning: our life and death is with the neighbor, the actual here and now context in which we live—including that unique neighbor who is my own embodied self and whom I must confront truthfully as I confront all the rest truthfully. Holiness doesn't begin tomorrow or over there or with that other person, and not with this person who stands before you. It doesn't begin with that other church, nor this one you know so well. One of the implications of what we have been thinking about is that we need to recognize the dangers of looking for the ideal church community (full of people like me), and to ask how I "pledge my body" to the Christian community I am actually with. Of course there are crises that can lead to tragic separation. Of course God leads us at times into new settings. However, for a very great deal of the time our difficulties are not to do with these questions of fundamental integrity but with the ordinary stresses of living with other equally unsatisfactory Christians. If you leave a church community too quickly, you find leaving becomes a habit; more saltwater to drink. Sooner or later you will have to confront the challenge of being pledged to uncomfortable reality—and of how to cope with that inner restlessness which constantly suggests what look like simpler solutions, avoiding the difficult route of changing yourself.

Many Christian churches now refer to those periods of the liturgical year when no great festivals or fasts are unfolding as Ordinary Time. It is a telling phrase; inevitably most of the time in the year is "ordinary"—yet all of it is the time won for us by Jesus Christ, all of it is gift, and in that sense extraordinary. It can never be strictly ordinary time, since it is the time in which day by day we are brought into the story, the drama, of God's action in Jesus. And the secret of living through the liturgical year lies in remembering the extraordinariness of the time that simply unfolds day after day, because it is the time in which we are constantly called and enabled to move and grow, in whatever circumstances face us. Here we are daily, not necessarily attractive and saintly people, along with other not very attractive and saintly people, managing the plain prose of our everyday service, deciding daily to recognize the prose of ourselves and each other as material for something unimaginably greater—the Kingdom of God, the glory of the saints, reconciliation and wonder. And we embody our decisions in both prayer and relation, inseparably, giving to both the attention they claim, so that together we begin to know ourselves found by God.

In the twentieth century there are still people who inhabit deserts of different kinds. They are those who have gone off on their own or have been taken into their form of the desert and so became for many others the touchstone of Christian integrity. I think here of Charles de Foucauld and his Little Brothers of Jesus, who explored their Christian calling both in the setting of the anonymous urban environment and literally in the desert. I think of the way in which other great figures like Thomas Merton and Bede Griffiths spoke from their desert after they had, in a sense, made themselves homeless by putting themselves on the edge of the conventional church and its ways. Both of them started out, you might say, as safe Catholic converts and good monks. Beginning as shaky

Catholic converts and becoming very unusual monks as
time went on, they entered a desert of not knowing any-
more where the external points of orientation were for
them and discovered within themselves what their map
was like. The Belgian Benedictine Henri Le Saux, Ab-
hishiktananda, was also a conventional monk before he
went off to India, to find that the landscape of his life was
dissolving and that he had to find something else within
another sort of desert.

I think equally of Dietrich Bonhoeffer in the desert
of his death cell, where he produced amazing material,
particularly his letters, which are among the great spiritual testimonies of the century. There is his wonderful
letter of May 1944, written for his godson's christening,
in which he writes of how easy it is for religious words
to become completely empty. It is not that he is merely a
liberal saying we ought to have easier and more up-to-
date religious words. That is actually the last thing he
wanted. His desert taught him that the old words are
there. They are real and solid, but we have abused them
so much that they have become stale, tired and rubbed
down, so much so that we do not know how to put con-
tent back into them. The only thing we can do, therefore,
is to take ourselves to prayer and action for justice. And
to say as little as we can.

There are many, too, who have been on the edges of
the church for the sake of the Kingdom. There are actives

and contemplatives and those who combine the two, like Desmond Tutu. We should look for the deserts today in the marginal places of the world and the church, and we should listen carefully to what's being said—or not said—there. I think there are many places to look for the successors of the desert fathers and mothers.

Then as today the cell, the place of staying, is a refining fire.

> A monk's cell is like the furnace in Babylon
> where the three young men found the Son of
> God. And it is like the pillar of cloud where
> God spoke to Moses.[14]

There is the rationale of staying in the cell, pledging the body and pledging to the body. Where we are and who we are is the furnace where the Son of God walks. When we begin to discover what contemplative faithfulness means, we recognize that we are in that furnace. Very, very occasionally, around an unexpected corner or with an unexpected person, we catch a glimpse of the fire, the desert filled with flame.

THE MONASTIC WISDOM
OF THE CHRISTIAN DESERT

A SELECTION OF SAYINGS

Laurence Freeman

The best way to understand someone is to meet the *person*. We meet the desert fathers and mothers in the rich collection of their sayings and stories that have been handed down in the Christian tradition for fifteen hundred years. This great collection of wisdom literature is a universal treasure, accessible to people of all traditions. One has only to read and ponder and read again. But this meeting is enhanced if we know something about the context in which this spiritual phenomenon appeared and flourished.

Christianity began as a Middle Eastern religious movement. The first church was in Jerusalem, and after the destruction of that mystical city in 70 A.D., Christianity diversified and radiated outward into North Africa and

Egypt. In great cultural centers like Rome, Alexandria, and Antioch, Christian thinkers began the process of theological exploration and dialogue not only with the biblical tradition of Jesus himself but more daringly with the philosophy of Greece.

But this development did not yet mean the separation of theology from prayer, of thought from experience. Indeed, the great fathers of the church, the founders of all Christian theological traditions and denominations, were almost without exception practitioners of the deep inner life of contemplation. They identified and celebrated the tension between the human need to speak about God and the impossibility of really doing so. The cataphatic tradition emphasized what could be said and needed to be thought about the mystery of God. But the apophatic tradition balanced this with its recognition of the unknowableness and the ineffability of God. This tension remains alive today wherever the richness of the Christian faith is lived. It provides the channel for the continuous transmission of wisdom that is the Christian mystical tradition. As the anonymous fourteenth-century English mystical work *The Cloud of Unknowing* puts it, "God cannot be known by thought but only by love." This saying captures the spirit of the Christian desert by stressing the identity of contemplation and love. Because, although the first Christian monastics, nonclerical men and women of all ages and backgrounds, were not intellectuals or academics, they were respected and acclaimed by their most intellectual contemporaries as true practitioners and explorers of the gospel.

Evagrius of Pontus, a fourth-century teacher of the desert, was an exception, a monk who was also an intellectual and a philosophical thinker. For that very reason he was at first an object of suspicion to the more rustic, uneducated, or even illiterate majority of desert monks. It was only after long testing in the asceticism of the monastic community that he won their affection, respect, and trust. When they said finally that he had gained the virtue of "discretion," they were awarding him a high honor. Evagrius knew well that a lack of education or sophistication was not necessarily a dearth of spiritual knowledge. Even the least literate monks knew the Bible by heart and understood its meanings on the pulse beat of their own experience. Their concern was transformative spiritual experience, not intellectual knowledge, and their primary means was to fulfill Saint Paul's injunction to "pray without ceasing" (1 THESS. 5:17). Not surprisingly, then, it is from Evagrius, a major source of Christian mystical theology about prayer, that we hear that "the one who prays is a theologian and the theologian is one who prays."

The process of institutionalizing the church accelerated after the emperor Constantine's establishment of Christianity as at first an officially tolerated and later the established religion of the Roman Empire. Yet the gospel ideals of union with Christ in the spirit, of purity of heart, and of an earthly society based on charity and forgiveness were not abandoned. The early church's anxious sense of the imminence of the Second Coming of Jesus (Rev. 22:20) that drove much of early Christian life gradually evolved into a concentration on lifestyles that would bring about an interior apocalypse. As the age of persecutions faded, the "white martyrdom" of prayer replaced it. The flight to the desert that was the birth of Christian monasticism meant a radical renunciation of personal wealth, family life, and the false glamour of fame and success, even when these took a spiritual form. Whether in remote single hermitages or in flexible gatherings of communities living in solitude together or in more regular forms of monastic community under a rule and an abbot, the fathers and mothers of the desert represented an affirmation and renewal of the purity and zeal of the Christian life. It was a movement of individuals responding to personal vocation but finding community through the solitude of their uniqueness.

The silence, fasting, and vigils, the struggle with one's inner demons, the celibacy and solitude of the desert, were all embraced as difficult but positive means of realizing the monastic goal. Extremism was rejected because it failed to achieve it. Pride in ascetical success was seen as a greater danger than failure, which could be more easily transcended by confession, humility, and forgiveness. A

feeding of the spirit on Scripture was not a biblical fundamentalism but an encounter with the spiritual power of
the sacred texts and an interiorization of their meaning at
the deepest level of perception. The life of the desert was
not a platonic abstraction. The body was disciplined, not
hated. Monks were not expected to be businessmen, but
they were not beggars either and were meant to earn their
daily bread by simple work like weaving baskets and mats
to be sold at market or even as seasonal farm laborers. But
because they lived so close to the cutting edge of matter
and spirit, body and soul, heaven and earth, they were seen
as special human beings, stewards of mysteries and medi-
ators for humanity. They themselves avoided such head-
lines, but it was the admiration of the more worldly
Christians that established the enduring influence of the
Christian desert.

The desert fathers and mothers were of all ages. A
few even brought their children with them. They might
come from wealthy or impoverished backgrounds. This
diversity helped develop the spirit of reasonableness, the
practice of the much-valued virtue of discretion, moderation, and flexibility in lifestyle, because as one story describes, what is a hard life for a former senator like
Arsenius is not much difficulty for a former shepherd.
Monks have always flourished on the margins of the religious institutions, and the weakness of contemporary
Christian monasticism is due to its having been so thor-

oughly institutionalized since the Middle Ages. Institutionalism in this context means clericalism. Not surprisingly then, we find the desert monks fleeing not only from the world but from clerical worldliness too. They avoided ordination even when asked to accept it as an honor or as a form of service. Consequently there is little overt concern with the sacramental life of the church in the stories of the desert.

The priority of the prayer of the heart, nourished by Scripture and a communal life of charity, is evident in the sixth-century Rule of Saint Benedict, the father of Western monasticism, which inherited and adapted the desert tradition and went on to embed it in Western society for a thousand years. This perennially adaptable rule of spiritual living can even be read as a commentary on the teachings of the desert fathers applied to life in community, as my remarks in the following selection of stories often suggest. At its height Christian desert monasticism in the early fourth century was said to have numbered ten thousand men and twenty thousand women. Most of them are unnamed, unknown pioneers and explorers of the spirit. But by the end of the fifth century, when this movement concluded under the pressures of marauding invasions and social change, a permanent entry had been inscribed in the Christian tradition and the religious culture of the human family. The spirit of the desert wisdom expanded far beyond Scetis and the Thebaid into Europe, through the *Conferences of the Fathers* of John Cassian and other texts.

Modern society is more indebted to the abbas and ammas of the desert than it might like to admit. Theirs was above all an oral tradition, and their teachings were first held and pondered in the heart of their disciples learning from their example. The spirit of this teaching was captured in the short sayings and stories that form the desert literature and that were written down, edited, and translated in a long process of transmission. We are the fortunate beneficiaries of this easily communicated and direct form of spiritual wisdom. We have only to listen and practice if we are to know what they knew.

CHARITY

The teaching of Jesus is summed up in the love of God and the love of neighbor as oneself. The wisdom of the desert saw charity (agape) as the core of its practice and both the means and the end of the spiritual life.

Anthony said, "Now I no longer fear God, I love him, for love casts out fear" (1 John 4:18).

He also said, "Our life and our death are with our neighbor. If we do good to our neighbor, we do good to God; if we cause our neighbor to stumble, we sin against Christ."

Agatho said, "I tried never to go to sleep while I kept a grievance against anyone. Nor did I let anyone go to sleep while he had a grievance against me."

One of the fathers said, "If anyone asks you for something, and you give it to him, even if you are forced to give it, let your heart go with the gift, as it is written, 'If a man forces you to go with him one mile, go with him two' (Matt. 5:41). This means that if you are asked for anything, give it with a willing heart."

It was said that a monk who had made baskets was putting handles on them when he heard another monk saying nearby, "What shall I do? The trader is coming soon and I haven't got any handles to put on my baskets." So he took off the handles he had put on his own baskets and took them to the nearby monk and said, "I don't need these; take them and put them on your baskets." He helped the brother to finish his baskets but left his own unfinished.

Two hermits lived together for many years without a quarrel. One said to the other, "Let's have a quarrel with each other, as other men do." The other answered, "I don't know how a quarrel happens." The first said, "Look here, I put a brick between us, and I say, 'That's mine.' Then you say, 'No, it's mine.' That is how you begin a quarrel." So they put a brick between them and one of them said, "That's mine." The other said, "No, it's mine." He answered, "Yes, it's yours. Take it away." They were unable to argue with each other.

A brother said to a hermit, "If I see a monk about whom I have heard that he is guilty of a sin, I cannot make myself invite him into my cell. But if I see a good monk, I bring him in gladly." The hermit said, "If you do good to a good brother, it is nothing to him, but to the other give double charity, for he is sick."

OPENING THE HEART

"How else but through a broken heart can Lord Christ enter in?" asked Oscar Wilde in the Ballad of Reading Goal. *The desert monastic wisdom gave high value to the experience of "*compunctio cordis,*" a painful but life-giving piercing of the heart that opens the whole person to the mystery of God in which we live and move and have our being. The real meaning of fear of God is discovered in this experience of radical self-judgment, not a fear of punishment, but the awe and wonder that arises in the presence of what is beyond our imagination and understanding.*

When Archbishop Theophilus of holy memory was dying, he said, "Arsenius, you are blessed of God, because you have always kept this moment before your eyes."

Jacob said, "Like a lantern giving light in a dark little room, so the fear of God comes into a man's heart and enlightens it, and teaches him all that is good and all the commandments of God."

DISCRETION

The desert monks were single-minded but not fanatic. Their admiration of discretion and their condemnation of those who spoke or acted without it show how deeply their practice was grounded in moderation and in a respect for the intricacies and relativity of the human condition. The humor of the desert is the sign and application of this discretion. It is not a corrosive cynical laughter but a corrective and instructive commentary on foolishness that avoided sanctimonious preaching or self-righteous judgmentalism.

They said of John the Short that he once said to his elder brother, "I want to be free of trouble like the angels, doing no work, and serving God unceasingly." He stripped himself and went into the desert. After a week there, he went back to his brother. When he knocked on the door, his brother answered without opening it and said, "Who's there?" He said, "It's John." His brother replied, "John has become an angel and is no longer among men." But he went on knocking and saying, "It really is John." His brother did not open the door but left him outside till morning as a punishment. At last he opened the door and said, "If you are a man, you need to work in order to live. If you are an angel, why do you want to come into my cell?" So John did penance and said, "Forgive me, brother."

Longinus asked Lucius, "I have three ideas, and the first is to go on a pilgrimage." He answered, "If you do not control your tongue, you will never be a pilgrim wherever you travel. But control your tongue here, and you will be a pilgrim, without traveling." Longinus said, "My second idea is to fast for two days at a time." Lucius answered, "The prophet Isaiah said, 'Even if you bend your neck to the ground, your fast will not so be accepted' (ISA. 58:5); you should rather guard your mind from evil thoughts." Longinus said, "My third idea is to avoid the company of men." Lucius answered, "Unless you first deal with your sins by living among men, you will not be able to deal with yourself when you live alone."

Poemen said, "Evil cannot drive out evil. If anyone hurts you, do good to him and your good will destroy his evil."

He also said, "A grumbler is not a monk. Anyone who gives evil for evil is not a monk. An irritable man is not a monk."

Hyperichius said, "He who teaches others by his life and not his speech is truly wise."

A hermit said, "Do not be pleased at everything that is said, and do not agree with everything that is said. Be slow to believe and quick to say what is true."

Some hermits used to say, "If you see a young man climbing up to heaven by his own will, catch him by the foot and pull him down to earth, for it is not good for him."

JUDGE NOT, THAT YOU BE NOT JUDGED

Aware of the fine balance needed for their life, the desert monks were particularly alert to the temptation and danger of superiority. They were astute enough to see the faults of others and wise enough to see the danger of condemning them. To condemn others is to imply and soon to believe that you are better than they. This sensitivity explains the importance given to the wisdom of the gospel teaching of Jesus not to judge others. There are other and more effective ways of helping people get over their faults. Both the life of the individual monk and the health of the community depended on this wisdom.

A brother sinned and the presbyter ordered him to go out of church. But Bessarion got up and went out with him, saying, "I too am a sinner."

When Isaac of the Thebaid visited a community, he saw that one of the brothers was sinful, and passed sentence on him. But when he was returning to his cell in the desert, the angel of the Lord came and stood in front of the door of his cell and said, "I will not let you go in." He asked, "Why not?" The angel of the Lord replied, "God sent me to ask you, 'Where do you tell me to send that sinful brother whom you sentenced?'" At once Isaac repented, saying, "I have sinned, forgive me." The angel said, "Get up, God has forgiven you. In future take care to judge no man before God has judged him."

A brother asked Poemen, "What am I to do, for I become weak just by sitting in my cell?" He said, "Despise no one, condemn no one, revile no one: and God will give you quietness, and you will sit at peace in your cell."

Once there was a meeting of monks in Scetis, and they discussed the case of a guilty brother, but Pior said nothing. Afterward he got up and went out, took a sack, filled it with sand, and carried it on his shoulders. He put a little sand in a basket and carried it in front of him. The monks asked him, "What are you doing?" He answered, "The sack with a lot of sand is my sins; they are many, so I put them on my back and then I shall not weep for them. The basket with a little sand is the sins of our brother, and they are in front of me, and I see them and judge them. This is not right. I ought to have my own sins in front of me, and think about them, and ask God to forgive me." When the monks heard this, they said, "This is the true way of salvation."

A hermit said, "Do not judge an adulterer if you are chaste or you will break the law of God just as much as he does. For he who said 'Do not commit adultery' also said 'Do not judge.'"

HUMILITY

Saint Benedict dedicates a whole chapter to humility in his Rule, and his twelve-step program for achieving it illustrates the influence of the desert tradition. False humility is a mutation of pride. The real thing is an expression of self-knowledge and of true relationship with others and the environment. These saying show the down-to-earthness of the really humble, as the etymology of the word itself suggests: humus *(earth).*

They said of Arsenius that while he was in the emperor's palace, he was the best-dressed person there, and while he was leading the life of a monk, no one was clothed in worse rags.

Arsenius once asked an old Egyptian monk for advice about his temptations. Another monk who saw this said, "Arsenius, how is it that you, who are so learned in Greek and Latin, are asking that uneducated peasant about your temptations?" He answered, "I have a lot of worldly knowledge of Greek and Latin, but I have not yet been able to learn the alphabet of this peasant."

The brothers in Scetis once met and began to discuss Melchizedek the priest, but they forgot to ask Copres to come. Later they summoned him and asked him what he thought about the question. He struck his mouth three times and said, "Alas for you, Copres. You have left undone what God commanded you to do, and you have dared to inquire into things that he did not ask of you." At these words the brothers scattered, each to his own cell.

Poemen said, "We ought always to be absorbing humility and the fear of God, as our nostrils breathe air in and out."

He also said, "Do not be proud of yourself, but stay with anyone who is living a good life."

He also said, "A brother asked Alonius, 'What is humility?' The hermit said, 'To be lower than brute beasts and to know that they are not condemned.'"

He also said, "Humility is the ground on which the Lord ordered the sacrifice to be offered."

Once Theophilus of holy memory, the archbishop of Alexandria, came to Scetis. The brothers gathered together and said to Pambo, "Speak to the bishop, that he may be edified." Pambo replied, "If he is not edified by my silence, my speech certainly will not edify him."

Syncletica of blessed memory said, "A ship cannot be built without nails, and no one can be saved without humility."

Hyperichius said, "The tree of life is high, and humility climbs it."

A hermit was asked, "What is humility?" He said, "It is if you forgive a brother who has wronged you before he is sorry."

ANONYMITY

The avoidance of fame and public adulation was part of the desert monks' lives. As word of the phenomenon spread, so did spiritual tourism, people who wanted proximity to the celebrity of the new spiritual heroes. If some of the lengths the monks went to in order to preserve their privacy and solitude seem amusing to us, this should not diminish our sense of the importance they attached to living in the light of God rather than the glare of publicity.

Anthony once heard about how a young monk showed off on a journey. He saw some old men walking wearily along the road, and he ordered some donkeys to appear and carry them home. When the old men told Anthony about this, he said, "I think that monk is like a ship laden with a rich cargo, but it is not yet certain that it will reach port in safety." Shortly afterward, Anthony began to weep and pull his hair and groan. When his disciples saw it, they said, "Why are you weeping, abba?" He replied, "A great pillar of the church has just fallen." He said this about the young monk, and added, "Walk over and see what has happened." So his disciples went, and found the monk sitting on his mat and weeping for a sin that he had committed. When he saw Anthony's disciples, he said, "Tell the abba to pray God to give me just ten days, and I hope to be able to satisfy him." Within five days he was dead.

The monks praised a brother to Anthony. Anthony went to him and tested him to see if he could endure being insulted. When he saw that he could not bear it, he said to him, "You are like a house with a highly decorated outside, but burglars have stolen all the furniture by the back door."

They said of Arsenius and Theodore of Pherme that they hated fame and praise more than anything. Arsenius avoided people likely to praise him. Theodore did not avoid them, but their words were like daggers to him.

Poemen also said, "Teach your heart to follow what your tongue is saying to others." He also said, "Men try to appear excellent in preaching, but they are less excellent in practicing what they preach."

Ammon (of the place called Raithu) brought this question to Sisoes: "When I read Scripture, I am tempted to make elaborate commentaries and prepare myself to answer questions on it." He replied, "You don't need to do that. It is better to speak simply, with a good conscience and a pure mind."

Once a provincial magistrate came to see Simon. Simon took off the leather belt that he wore and climbed a palm tree to clean it with the palm leaves. When the judge's party came up, they said, "Where is the hermit of this desert?" Simon answered, "There is no hermit here." So the judge went away.

Another time a magistrate came to see him, and the clergy who went on ahead said to him, "Abba, get ready, for the judge has heard of you and is coming to be blessed by you." So he covered himself with sackcloth, and took bread and cheese in his hand, and sat down in his doorway and began to eat it. The magistrate arrived with his retinue. When they saw him, they despised him and said, "Is this the hermit about whom we heard such great things?" They turned around and went straight home.

Syncletica said, "An open treasury is quickly spent; any virtue will be lost if it is published abroad and is known about everywhere. If you put wax in front of a fire, it melts; and if you pour vain praises on the soul, it goes soft and weak in seeking goodness."

She also said, "The same thing cannot at once be seed and a full-grown bush. So men with a worldly reputation cannot bear heavenly fruit."

Once at a feast day in Cellia the brothers were eating their meal in church. But one of them said to the server, "I eat nothing cooked, only salted." The serving monk called to another brother in front of the whole crowd, "This brother doesn't eat what is cooked, bring him the salt." But one of the brothers stood up and said to him, "It would have been better for you to eat meat today in your cell than to have heard this said in front of many brothers."

MODESTY

Modesty is not a virtue of the modern media culture, but it was central to the lived humility of the desert. Having nothing to do with self-denigration in a destructive sense, it had everything to do with preserving the freshness of contact with the original motivation for entering this way of life.

A brother said to Sisoes, "I want to guard my heart." He said to him, "How can we guard the heart if our tongue leaves the door of the fortress open?"

Moses asked Silvanus, "Can a monk live every day as though it were the first day of his monastic life?" Silvanus answered, "If you are truly committed to your way of life, you can live every day, every hour, as though it were the first day or hour of your monastic life."

Syncletica said, "Let us live soberly, for thieves get in through our bodily senses. The inside of the house is sure to be blackened if the smoke that is coiling up outside finds the windows open."

A hermit said, "Unless the inner self lives soberly, the outer self is beyond control."

HOSPITALITY

Saint Benedict shows his roots in desert spirituality by the importance he gives to hospitality. The monastery, he said, would never be without guests, and every guest, however inconvenient, should be welcomed as Christ himself. Even in the hermitages of the desert, the desert monks understood and practiced this essential Christian sense of the divinity of one's neighbor.

Cassian said, "We came from Palestine to Egypt and visited one of the hermits. After he had welcomed us, we asked him, 'When you receive guests, why don't you fast? In Palestine they do.' He answered, 'Fasting is always possible, but I cannot keep you here forever. Fasting is useful and necessary, but we can choose to fast or not fast. God's law demands from us perfect love. I receive Christ when I receive you, so I must do all I can to show you love. When I have said good-bye to you, I can take up my rule of fasting again. "The sons of the bridegroom cannot fast while the bridegroom is with them; when he is taken from them, then they can fast"'" (Matt. 9:15).

In Scetis there once went out an order that they should fast for a week and then celebrate Easter. During the week some brothers happened to come into Egypt to visit Moses, and he cooked a little vegetable stew for them. The nearby hermits saw the smoke and said to the clergy of the church, "What is that smoke? Moses must be disobeying the order and cooking in his cell." The clergy said, "We will talk to him when he comes." On Saturday the clergy, who knew the greatness of his way of life, said to Moses in front of the whole congregation, "Moses, you have broken a commandment of men, but you have kept the commandments of God valiantly."

A brother came to Poemen in the second week of Lent and told him his thoughts, and found peace of mind from his answer. Then he said, "I almost didn't come to see you today." Poemen asked him why. He said, "I was afraid that the door wouldn't be opened as it is Lent." Poemen answered him, "It is not wooden doors we were taught to shut; the door we need to keep shut is the mouth."

OBEDIENCE

Solitude is the basis of relationship, and obedience is the fruit of all authentic relation. In the obedience theme of the desert sayings, we can hear echoes of the Zen masters and their training of disciples in the art of obedience. Saint Benedict once again offers a commentary on the desert wisdom in his approach to obedience, one of the three precepts still taken by Benedictine monks today. Vertical obedience to a superior—doing what you are told without inner grumbling or delay—is an ascesis of the will. But like all virtues, it is governed by discretion (the "mother of all virtues"). The psychological healthiness of vertical obedience is tested by the horizontal obedience of all members of the community to each other. Thus all become mutually obedient—the word comes from the Latin for "to listen"—in a collective attunement to the Word of God sounding in their hearts and in their midst.

They told this story of John the Short. He went to live with a hermit from the Thebaid, who was living in the desert of Scetis. His abba once took a dead stick and planted it, and told him, "Pour a jug of water over its base every day until it bears fruit." Water was so far from their cell that John had to go off every evening to fetch it, and it was dawn before he returned. At the end of three years the stick turned green and bore fruit. The hermit picked some of the fruit and took it to church, and said to the brothers, "Take and eat the fruit of obedience."

They said of John, the disciple of Paul, that he was full of the virtue of obedience. There was a tomb in which lived a dangerous lioness. Paul saw the dung of the lioness lying around and said to John, "Go and fetch that dung." John said to him, "What shall I do, abba, about the lioness?" The hermit said, as a joke, "If she comes at you, tie her up and bring her here." So John went there in the evening, and the lioness rushed at him. He obeyed the hermit and ran to catch her, so the lioness turned and fled. John chased her, shouting, "Wait! My abba told me to tie you up." He caught her and tied her up. The hermit sat a long time waiting for him, and was getting very anxious because he was late. But at last John came, and brought the lioness with him, tied up. Paul marveled at the sight. But wanting to humble him, he beat him and said, "You fool, have you brought me that silly dog?" and he immediately untied her and drove her away.

Syncletica said, "It seems to me that for those who live in monasteries, obedience is a higher virtue than chastity, however perfect. Chastity is in danger of pride; obedience has the promise of humility."

PATIENCE

Endurance, fidelity, is the condition of all growth. In the story of Evagrius, we feel the price of this to the sensitivity of the ego. It also became for the desert monks the sure test that the long years of spiritual practice had borne fruit in the sweetness and gentleness of old age.

At a meeting of the hermits in Cellia, Evagrius made a speech. Then the priest there said, "Evagrius, we know that if you were in your own country, perhaps you would already be a bishop, ruling over many. Here you are only a pilgrim." Evagrius was pierced to the heart at these words, but he bent his head calmly and without haste and looked at the ground, then wrote in the dust with his finger, and said, "Truly, brothers, that is right. But, as it is written, 'I have spoken once and I will no more answer'" (Job 40:5).

John the Less of the Thebaid, a disciple of Ammon, was said to have lived for twelve years serving a hermit who was ill, sitting on a mat near him. But the hermit was always cross with him, and although John worked a long time for him, he never said, "May it be well with you." But when the hermit was on his deathbed, in the presence of the brothers of the place, he held John's hand and said,

"May it be well with you, may it be well with you." The hermit commended John to the others, saying, "He is an angel, not a man."

They said of Isidore, the priest in Scetis, that if anyone had a monk who was sick or weak or insolent and wanted to send him away, he would say, "Bring him to me." Then he would take him and cure him by his patience.

POSSESSING NOTHING

To those in the know, poverty is the secret luxury of monastic life. Free from material anxiety and the complications of ownership, the monk can enjoy everything or be happy with nothing. But as Syncletica, one of the great mothers of the desert, suggests, poverty needs to be situated within the whole economy of the virtues. Just as a proud virgin is less than a humble profligate, so poverty needs to be seen not merely in terms of things but of fundamental attitudes and nonpossessiveness.

Evagrius said that there was a brother who had no possessions except a Gospel book, and he sold it in order to feed the poor. He said something worth remembering: "I have sold even the word that commands me to sell all and give to the poor."

Cassian said that Syncleticus renounced the world and divided his property among the poor. But he kept some for his own use, and so he showed that he was unwilling to accept either the poverty of those who renounce everything or the normal rule of monasteries. Basil of blessed memory said to him, "You have stopped being a senator, but you have not become a monk."

A brother said to Pistamon, "What am I to do? I am anxious when I sell what I make." Pistamon replied, "Sisoes and others used to sell what they made. There is no harm in this. When you sell anything, say straight away the price of the goods. If you want to lower the price a little, you may, and so you will find peace." The brother said, "I have enough for my needs from other sources, do you think I need worry about making things to sell?" Pistamon answered, "However much you have, do not stop making things; do as much as you can, provided that your soul is at peace."

A brother said to Serapion, "Give me a word." But he replied, "What can I say to you? You have taken what belongs to widows and orphans and put it on your window ledge." He saw that the window ledge was full of books.

Syncletica of blessed memory was asked, "Is absolute poverty perfect goodness?" She replied, "It is a great good for those who can do it. Even those who cannot bear it find rest to their souls though they suffer bodily anxiety. As strong clothes are laundered pure white by being turned and trodden underfoot in water, a strong soul is strengthened by freely accepting poverty."

Syncletica said, "Merchants toil in search of riches and are in danger of their lives from shipwreck; the more wealth they win, the more they want, and they think what they have already is of no worth but bend their whole mind to what they have not yet got. But we have nothing, not even that which we ought to seek; we do not even want to possess what we need, because we fear God."

SELF-CONTROL

For Saint Paul, self-control is one of the nine fruits of the Spirit (GAL. 5:22). The practices of all the paths of the virtues in the desert wisdom depend on this basic skill. As Dioscorus illustrates below, it is a capacity best developed in a systematic way until it becomes second nature.

They said of Ammoi that though he was ill in a bed for several years, he never relaxed his discipline and never went to the store cupboard at the back of his cell to see what was in it. Many people brought him presents because he was ill. But even when his disciple, John, went in and out, he shut his eyes so as not to see what he was doing. He knew what it means to be a faithful monk.

They said that Dioscorus of Namisias made his bread out of barley and his soup out of lentils. Every year he made one particular resolution: either not to meet anyone for a year, or not to speak, or not to taste cooked food, or not to eat any fruit, or not to eat vegetables. This was his system in everything. He made himself master of one thing, and then started on another, and so on each year.

Evagrius quoted a hermit as saying, "I cut away bodily pleasure in order to get rid of occasions for anger; I know that it is because of pleasure that I have to struggle with anger, my mind being disturbed and my understanding disordered."

The holy Syncletica said, "We who have chosen this holy way of life ought above all to preserve chastity. Even among men of the world, chastity is highly regarded. But in the world they are also stupid about it, and sin with their other senses. For they peep indecently, and laugh immoderately."

Sisoes said, "Our form of pilgrimage is keeping the mouth closed."

Lust
As desert conditions offered limited opportunities for sexual activity, the struggle with the untransformed desires of sexuality was

often against erotic fantasy. Nothing shows the balance and health of the desert mothers and fathers better than their attitude toward sex, seeing it as they did as a force needing to be faced, integrated, and transformed rather than repressed.

Poemen said, "As a bodyguard is always standing by to protect the emperor, so the soul should always be ready to fight the demon of lust."

They said of Sarah that for thirteen years she was fiercely attacked by the demon of lust. She never prayed that the battle should leave her, but she used to say only, "Lord, give me strength."

They also said of her that the same demon of lust was once attacking her threateningly, tempting her with vain thoughts of the world. She continued in the fear of God and maintained the rigor of her fasting. Once when she climbed up on the roof to pray, the spirit of lust appeared to her in bodily form and said to her, "You have overcome me, Sarah." But she replied, "It is not I who have overcome you, but my Lord Christ."

A brother was obsessed by lust, and it was like a fire burning day and night in his heart. But he struggled on, not examining the temptation nor consenting to it. After a long time, the fire left him, extinguished by his perseverance.

A hermit said, "Chastity is born of tranquillity and silence and inner prayer."

STICKING WITH IT

Perseverance is a virtue often advocated by Saint Paul, the Christian capacity to endure hard times with faith and hope and charity. In the desert wisdom, we see that this gift is the bottom line of all spiritual endeavor. It empowers one to get through those tunnels of life in which understanding or enthusiasm in the spiritual path are temporarily eclipsed. It is also related to the sense of humor without which mere endurance would become fanaticism.

This same Macarius once went down from Scetis to a place named Terenuthis, and he climbed into an old pagan burial place to sleep. He put one of the bodies under his head as a pillow. The demons hated him when they saw his assurance and tried to frighten him by calling out, "Lady, come with us to bathe." Another demon answered from underneath Macarius, as though he were the dead woman, "I have a pilgrim on top of me, and can't move." Macarius was not frightened but confidently thumped the body, saying, "Get up and go if you can." When the demons heard it, they cried out and said, "You have defeated us," and they fled in confusion.

Syncletica said, "If you live in a monastic community, do not wander from place to place; if you do, it will harm you. If a hen stops sitting on the eggs, she will hatch no chickens. The monk or nun who goes from place to place grows cold and dead in faith."

She also said, "The devil sometimes sends a severe fast that is too prolonged; the devil's disciples do this as well as holy men. How do we distinguish the fasting of our God and King from the fasting of that tyrant the devil? Clearly by its moderation. Throughout your life, then, you ought to keep an unvarying rule of fasting. Do you fast four or five days on end and then lose your spiritual strength by eating a feast? That really pleases the devil! Everything that is extreme is destructive. So do not suddenly throw away your armor, or you may be found unarmed in the battle and easily captured. Our body is the armor, our soul is the warrior. Take care of both, and you will be ready for whatever comes."

A hermit said, "If you fall ill, do not complain. If the Lord God has willed that your body should be weakened, who are you to complain about it? Does he not care for you in all your needs? Surely you would not be alive without him. Be patient in your illness and ask God to give you what is right, that is, that which will enable you to do his will, and be patient, and eat what you have in charity."

The Overview

The monastic literature frequently returns to a general overview of the monk's long-term task. This bird's-eye view provided perspective, encouragement, and a refreshment of the integrated sense of the whole life project. We see in the following sayings the general economy of the desert virtues and the ideal of the monk as a man or woman in whom an integrated personality was continuously evolving.

They used to say about Theodore of Pherme that he kept these three rules before all others: poverty, abstinence, and avoiding the company of other people.

John the Short said, "I will invent a man composed of all the virtues. He would rise at dawn every morning, take up the beginning of each virtue, and keep God's commandments. He would live in great patience, in fear, in long-suffering, in love of God; with a firm purpose of soul and body; in deep humility, in patience, in trouble of heart and earnestness of practice. He would pray often, with sorrow of heart, keeping his speech pure, his eyes controlled. He would suffer injury without anger, remaining peaceful and not rendering evil for evil, not looking out for the faults of others, nor puffing himself up, meekly subject to every creature, renouncing material property and everything of the flesh. He would live as though crucified, in struggle, in lowliness of spirit, in goodwill and spiritual abstinence, in fasting, in penitence, in weeping. He would fight against evil, be wise and discreet in judgment and chaste in mind. He would receive good treatment with tranquillity, working with his own hands, watching at night, enduring hunger and thirst, cold and nakedness and labor. He would live as though buried in a tomb and already dead, every day feeling death to be near him."

Joseph of Thebes said, "Three things are seen to be honorable by God. The first is when temptations come on someone who is weak and are accepted thankfully. The second is when every action is pure before God, mixed with no human motive. The third is when a disciple remains obedient to a spiritual father and gives up all his self-will."

Sisoes said, "Be despised; put your self-will behind your back; be free of worldly concerns, and you will have peace."

When Chame was dying, he said to his sons, "Do not live with heretics. Do not take any notice of judges. Do not open your hands to get, but let them be stretched out to give."

A brother said to a hermit, "How does the fear of God come into the soul?" He said, "If there is humility and poverty, and no judgment of others, the fear of God will be present there."

Some of the hermits used to say, "Whatever you hate for yourself, do not do it to someone else. If you hate being spoken evil of, do not speak evil of another. If you hate being slandered, do not slander another. If you hate him who tries to make you despised, or wrongs you, or takes away what is yours, or anything like that, do not do such things to others. To keep this is enough for salvation."

A hermit said, "This is the life of a monk: work, obedience, meditation, not to judge others, not to speak evil, not to murmur. For it is written, 'You who love God, hate the thing that is evil' (Ps. 97:10). This is monastic life: not to live with the wicked, not to see evil, not to be inquisitive, not to be curious, not to listen to gossip, not to use the hands for taking but for giving, not to be proud in heart or bad in thought, not to fill the belly, in everything to judge wisely. That is the life of the true monk."

PROPHETIC VISIONS

The desert elders warned strongly (as do their peers in all traditions) against expecting, seeking, or advertising psychic powers. Yet at times we see in these stories examples of their refined powers of perception and how they accepted or used them in ways conditioned by all the virtues illustrated above, especially in moderation, charity, and humility.

It happened that Moses, who lived in Petra, was struggling with the temptation to fornication. Unable to stay any longer in the cell, he went and told Isidore about it. He advised him to return to his cell. But he refused, saying, "Abba, I cannot." Then Isidore took Moses out onto the terrace and said to him, "Look toward the west." He looked and saw hordes of demons standing about and making a noise before launching an attack. Then Isidore said to him, "Look toward the east." He turned and saw an innumerable multitude of holy angels shining with glory. Isidore said, "See, these are sent by the Lord to the saints to bring them help, while those in the west fight against them. Those who are with us are more in number than they are against us" [cf. 2 Kings 6:16]. So Moses gave thanks to God, plucked up courage, and returned to his cell.

One day when the brothers were sitting near him, Macarius said to them, "Look, the barbarians are coming to Scetis today; get up and flee." They said to him, "Abba, won't you flee too?" He said to them, "I've been

waiting for many years for this day when the word of
Christ will be fulfilled, 'They who take the sword shall
perish by the sword'" [Matt. 26:52]. They said to him,
"We will not flee either, we will die with you." He
replied, "That's nothing to do with me; let each one decide for himself if he will stay or flee." There were seven
brothers there and he said to them, "Look, the barbarians
are nearly at the door," and they came in and slew them.
But one of them fled and hid under a pile of rope, and
he saw seven crowns coming down and crowning each
of them.

John, who had been exiled by the emperor Marcian, said,
"One day we went into Syria to see Poemen, for we
wanted to ask him about hardness of heart. But he did not
know Greek and we did not have an interpreter. When he
saw we were embarrassed, he began to speak in Greek,
saying, 'The nature of water is soft, the nature of stone is
hard, but if a bottle is hung above a stone letting water
drip down, it wears away the stone. It is like that with the
word of God; it is soft and our heart is hard, but if a man
hears the word of God often, it will break open his heart
to the fear of God.'"

Silence
*Silence is the laboratory of the spirit, the labor of prayer. It is also
the fruit of practice, because as Meister Eckhart said, "There is*

nothing so much like God as silence." However important it is, the less said about silence, obviously, the better.

Anthony said, "He who sits alone and is quiet has escaped from three wars: hearing, speaking, seeing, but there is one thing against which he must continually fight: that is, his own heart."

Arsenius, when he was still in the palace, prayed to God, saying, "Lord, show me the way of salvation." A voice came to him saying, "Arsenius, flee from men and you will be saved." As he left for the monastic life, he prayed again, saying the same words, and he heard a voice saying to him, "Arsenius, flee, be silent, pray always, for these are the roots of sinlessness."

Evagrius said, "Cut the desire for many things out of your heart and so prevent your mind from being dispersed and your stillness lost."

In Scetis a brother went to Moses to ask for advice. He said to him, "Go and sit in your cell, and your cell will teach you everything."

Nilus said, "The arrows of the enemy cannot touch someone who loves quiet. But those who wander about among crowds will often be wounded by them."

Continuous Prayer

If the motives of the desert mothers and fathers could be summed up in one aspiration, it would be to come to the state of continuous prayer. Saint Benedict recognizes this when he describes the structure of daily prayers in community as leading to an awakening of the prayer heart. As these final sayings show, such prayer is not a matter of words or forms but an opening of consciousness to the life of the spirit flowing in the present moment of God, the making of our mind to be one with the mind of Christ: not only to pray, then, but to become prayer.

Bishop Epiphanius of Cyprus, of holy memory, was told this by the abbot of his monastery in Palestine. "By your prayers we have kept our rule; we carefully observe the offices of terce, sext, none, and vespers." But Epiphanius rebuked him and said, "Then you are failing to pray at other times. The true monk ought to pray without ceasing [1 THESS. 5:17]. He should always be singing psalms in his heart."

Isaiah said, "A priest at Pelusium was holding a love feast, and when the brothers in church were eating and talking, he rebuked them saying, 'Be quiet, my brothers. There is one brother eating among you whose prayer is going up to God like a darting flame.'"

Lot went to Joseph and said, "Abba, as far as I can, I keep a moderate rule, with a little fasting, and prayer, and meditation, and quiet, and as far as I can, I try to cleanse my heart of evil thoughts. What else should I do?" Then the hermit stood up and spread out his hands to heaven, and his fingers shone like ten flames of fire, and he said "If you will, you can become all flame."

Some brothers asked Macarius, "How should we pray?" He said, "There is no need to talk much in prayer. Reach out your hands often and say, 'Lord have mercy on me, as you will and as you know.' But if conflict troubles you, say, 'Lord, help me.' He knows what is best for us and has mercy."

A hermit used to say, "Ceaseless prayer soon heals the mind."

NOTES

CHAPTER 1 LIFE, DEATH, AND NEIGHBORS

1. Ward, Benedicta, trans. *The Sayings of the Desert Fathers* (Kalamazoo, Mich.: Cistercian, 1984), 3; cf. the saying ascribed to him in Athanasius's *Life of Anthony* 67, which confirms the authenticity of this tradition.

2. Ward. *The Sayings of the Desert Fathers*, 141.

3. Ward. *The Sayings of the Desert Fathers*, 141. The implication is that without this, no one can rightly see himself or herself as a sinner.

4. Ward. *The Sayings of the Desert Fathers*, 93.

5. Ward. *The Sayings of the Desert Fathers*, 102.

6. Ward. *The Sayings of the Desert Fathers*, 134.

7. Ward. *The Sayings of the Desert Fathers*, 134; cf. Macarius 21, on Macarius's reaction to the severe discipline of another abba.

8. Ward. *The Sayings of the Desert Fathers*, 169; cf. Sisoes 20 for a closely similar story.

9. Ward. *The Sayings of the Desert Fathers*, 126; cf. Poemen 62, offers a good example of both identification with the sinner and modification of another's harshness:

Poemen tells the questioning monk that his previous adviser has his thoughts in heaven, while "you and I" still suffer from sexual temptation. See also Poemen 6 for a rebuke to a hermit for judging harshly.

10. Ward. *The Sayings of the Desert Fathers*, 138–39.

11. Anon. 123.

12. Ward. *The Sayings of the Desert Fathers*, 42.

13. Ward. *The Sayings of the Desert Fathers*, 134.

14. Ward. *The Sayings of the Desert Fathers*, 175; cf. Anon. 186 for a slightly more complex response, but with the same concern to nurture humility.

15. Ward. *The Sayings of the Desert Fathers*, 180.

16. Ward. *The Sayings of the Desert Fathers*, 142; cf. Poemen 6.

17. Ward. *The Sayings of the Desert Fathers*, 184.

18. On the whole scapegoat impulse, see the works of René Girard and James Alison, especially Girard's *Things Hidden Since the Foundation of the World* (London: Athlone, 1987), and Alison's *Raising Abel* (New York: Crossroad Publishing, 1996).

19. Ward. *The Sayings of the Desert Fathers*, 2.

20. John the Dwarf 13; cf. Anon. 38.

21. See, for example, Dioscorus 2.

22. See the sayings in Anon. 132–48. For the importance of nepsis in later literature, see the treatise on the subject by Hesychios the Priest (probably eighth century or a little later) included in the *Philokalia* (ed. and trans. by G. E. H. Palmer, P. Sherrard, and K. Ware, vol. 1 [Lon-

don: Faber and Faber, 1979], pp. 162–98). The whole of the *Philokalia* is described as the work of the "watchful" fathers.

23. See especially Graham Gould, *The Desert Fathers on Monastic Community* (Oxford: Clarendon Press, 1993), and Douglas Burton-Christie, *The Word in the Desert* (New York: Oxford University Press, 1993), chaps. 8 and 9.

CHAPTER 2 SILENCE AND HONEY CAKES

1. Ward. *The Sayings of the Desert Fathers*, 17–18.
2. Arsenius 2, 4, 25, 42.
3. Ward. *The Sayings of the Desert Fathers*, 6; cf. the more obviously pious variant preserved in the Alphabetical Collection under the name of Eucharistos.
4. Anon. 84.
5. Augustine, *De natura et gratia* 29.33.
6. Arsenius 36.
7. For example, Theodora 6; cf. Macarius 11 and 35.
8. Evagrius 7.
9. Ward. *The Sayings of the Desert Fathers*, 81.
10. Annie Dillard, *The Writing Life* (New York: Harper and Row, 1989), p. 52.
11. Ibid., p. 4.
12. Ward. *The Sayings of the Desert Fathers*, 90.
13. Ward. *The Sayings of the Desert Fathers*, 98.
14. Henri de Lubac, *Paradoxes of Faith* (San Francisco: Ignatius Press, 1987), pp.122, 127.

15. Ward. *The Sayings of the Desert Fathers*, 181.

16. Theodore of Pherme 9.

17. John Chryssavgis, *In the Heart of the Desert* (Blooming-ton, Ind.: World Wisdom, 2003), p. 76.

18. Raymond Plant, *Politics, Theology, and History* (Cam-bridge: Cambridge University Press, 2001), chaps. 11 and 12.

19. Lossky's fullest exposition of these themes can be found in the posthumous collection of his essays *In the Image and Likeness of God* (Crestwood, N.Y.: St. Vladimir's Seminary Press, 1974), especially chaps. 6 and 7, and in the postscript to another posthumous volume, edited from transcripts of lectures in Paris, *Orthodox Theology: An Introduction* (Crestwood, N.Y.: St. Vladimir's Seminary Press, 1978), pp. 119–37.

20. See particularly the works of Lossky's pupil Olivier Clèment, for example, *Questions sur l'homme*, 2nd ed. (Sainte-Foy, Quebec: Éditions A. Sigier, 1986), and *La révolte de l'esprit* (Paris: Stock, 1979), and that of the Greek theologian Christos Yannaras, for example, *The Freedom of Morality* (Crestwood, N.Y.: St. Vladimir's Seminary Press, 1984).

21. There are many discussions in the *Philokalia* texts of the phenomenology of temptation and of the sense in which Christ is truly tempted: see, for example, Hesy-chios, "On Watchfulness and Holiness" 46 in *Philokalia*, vol. 1, pp. 170–71, and John Damascene, "On the Virtues and the Vices" in *Philokalia*, vol. 2 (London: Faber and Faber, 1981), pp. 337–38.

CHAPTER 3 FLEEING

1. Ward. *The Sayings of the Desert Fathers*, 74.

2. Ward. *The Sayings of the Desert Fathers*, 9.

3. Ward. *The Sayings of the Desert Fathers*, 133.

4. Ward. *The Sayings of the Desert Fathers*, 2.

5. These thoughts are discussed at length by Evagrius and Cassian; see vol. 1 of the *Philokalia*, pp. 38–52 and 73–93.

6. For example, Cronius 5, an anecdote about a monk who had been a senior civil servant and in the desert distinguished himself by his lack of concern for his personal appearance.

7. For example, Macarius 16.

8. Macarius 41: "Flee from human company, stay in your cell, weep for your sins, and don't take pleasure in human conversation, and then you will be saved."

9. Cassian, *Institutes* 11.18.

10. Ward. *The Sayings of the Desert Fathers*, 77; cf. Isaac of the Cells 1 and Peter of Dios 1.

11. Joseph of Panephysis 7; (cf. Joseph of Panephysis 6, a more prosaic version of what is obviously the same tradition).

12. Poemen 8; a visitor tries to discuss "heavenly things" with Poemen, who responds only when the guest begins to ask advice about the passions of the soul. This echoes Poemen 62 (see chap. 1, n 9.); cf. Anthony 17, the commendation of Abba Joseph for saying "I don't know" when asked about the meaning of a text.

13. Ward. *The Sayings of the Desert Fathers*, 131.

14. Macarius 14.

15. Dillard, *Writing Life*, p. 10.

16. See, for an overview, "Language and Propaganda" in *The Thomas Merton Encyclopaedia*, ed. William Shannon, Christine Bochen, and Patrick O'Connell (Maryknoll, N.Y.: Orbis Books, 2002), pp. 242–44.

17. This idea is especially important in Maximus the Confessor and has been used in the modern period by the Romanian theologian Dumitru Staniloae; see Charles Miller, *The Gift of the World: An Introduction to the Theology of Dumitru Staniloae* (Edinburgh: T and T Clark, 2000), pp. 60–62.

18. Mercedes Pavlicevic, *Music Therapy: Intimate Notes* (London: Jessica Kingsley Publishers, 1999), especially pp. 20–21.

19. John the Dwarf 2; Theodore of Pherme 15, 28.

20. See, for example, Simone Weil, *Intimations of Christianity among the Ancient Greeks* (London: Routledge and Kegan Paul, 1957), pp. 24–55, on power as what stands in the way of reflection, hesitation, in the presence of another person. For a fine discussion, see Peter Winch, *Simone Weil: "The Just Balance"* (Cambridge: Cambridge University Press, 1989), pp. 107–8, 164 ff.

21. For example, Isaac of the Cells 2; Poemen 73, 174; Sisoes 45.

22. Bessarion 10.

23. Ward. *The Sayings of the Desert Fathers*, 110.

Chapter 4 Staying

1. Ward. *The Sayings of the Desert Fathers*, 231.

2. Ward. *The Sayings of the Desert Fathers*, 139.

3. Ward. *The Sayings of the Desert Fathers*, 95.

4. See also chap. 3, n. 5.

5. Rule of Saint Benedict, chap. 1.

6. Anon. 68.

7. Anon. 69.

8. Anon. 63; cf. Arsenius 11 for a shorter version.

9. Dillard, *Writing Life*, p. 26.

10. Anon. 76.

11. Anon. 73.

12. Søren Kierkegaard, *Philosophical Fragments, Johannes Climacus,* ed. and trans. Howard Hong and Edna Hong (Princeton, N.J.: Princeton University Press, 1985), p. 55: "From the hour when by the omnipotent resolution of his omnipotent love he became a servant, he has himself become captive, so to speak, in his resolution and is now obliged to continue (to go on talking loosely) whether he wants to or not."

13. Ward. *The Sayings of the Desert Fathers*, 234.

14. Anon. 74.

FURTHER READING

BOOKS

Primary Sources in Translation

Ward, Benedicta, trans. *The Sayings of the Desert Fathers:*
 The Alphabetical Collection. London: Mowbrays, 1975.
———. *The Wisdom of the Desert Fathers: The Apophthegmata*
 Patrum (the anonymous series). Oxford: S.L.G. Press,
 1975.

Significant Recent Studies

Burton-Christie, Douglas. *The Word in the Desert: Scripture*
 and the Quest for Holiness in Early Christian Monasticism.
 New York: Oxford University Press, 1993.

Chryssavgis, John. *In the Heart of the Desert: The Spirituality*
 of the Desert Fathers and Mothers. Bloomington, Ind.:
 World Wisdom, 2003.

Gould, Graham. *The Desert Fathers on Monastic Community.*
 Oxford: Clarendon Press, 1993.

Ramfos, Stelios. *Like a Pelican in the Wilderness: Reflections on*
 The Sayings of the Desert Fathers. Brookline, Mass.: Holy
 Cross Orthodox Press, 2000.

Starowieyski, Marek, ed. *The Spirituality of Ancient Monasticism: Acts of the International Colloquium Held at Cracow-Tyniec 1994.* Tyniec, Poland: Wydawn. Benedyktynow, 1995 (especially J. Pollok, "The Present State of Studies on the *Apophthegmata Patrum:* An Outline of Samuel Rubenson's and Graham Gould's Perspectives," pp.79–89).

Stewart, Columba. *Cassian the Monk.* New York: Oxford University Press, 1998.

———. "The Desert Fathers on Radical Honesty about the Self." *Sobornost* 12 (1990): 25–39, 131–56; reprint *Vox Bendictina* 8 (1991): 7–53.

RECORDING

Williams, R. "The Wisdom of the Desert: The John Main Seminar 2001." Tucson, Ariz.: Medio Media, 2002.

THE WORLD COMMUNITY
FOR CHRISTIAN MEDITATION
AND THE JOHN MAIN SEMINAR

The World Community for Christian Meditation is a contemplative community founded in the inspiration of the Benedictine monk John Main (1926–1982), who was a major influence in the contemporary recovery of the contemplative Christian tradition. The community is composed of individuals and groups following the teaching on meditation taught in the desert tradition. Weekly Christian Meditation groups meet in sixty countries and about thirty Christian Meditation centers around the world. An international center in England coordinates many aspects of the life of the community, which include the annual John Main Seminar, an international schedule of retreats and seminars, a school for the training of teachers of Christian Meditation, and the development of religious education programs to include meditation, a quarterly newsletter, and a Web site: www.wccm.org.

Christian Meditation Center of California
2975 Huntingdon Dr., Suite 1000
San Marino, CA 91108-2223
Phone: 626-793-3775

WCCM USA National Center
627 N. 6th Ave.
Tucson, AZ 85705
Phone: 1-800-324-8305

WCCM International Centre
Saint Mark's
Myddelton Square
London EC1R 1XX, UK
Email: mail@wccm.org
Phone: 44-020-7278-2070

Medio Media is the publishing arm of The World Community for Christian Meditation. The online bookstore is www.mediomedia.org.

For a catalog or phone orders:

Medio Media
627 N. 6th Ave.
Tucson, AZ 85705
Phone: 1-800-324-8305

THE JOHN MAIN SEMINAR 1984–2005

1984 Isabelle Glover: Indian Scriptures as Christian Spiritual Reading

1985 Robert Kiely: The Search for God in Modern Literature

1986 John M. Todd: The New Church

1987 Derek Smith: On Reading

1988 Charles Taylor: Christian Identity and Modernity

1989 Balfour Mount: On Wholeness

1990 Eileen O'Hea: Spirit and Psyche

1991 Bede Griffiths: Christian Meditation—An Evolving
      Tradition

1992 Jean Vanier: From Brokenness to Wholeness

1993 William Johnston: The New Christian Mysticism

1994 The Dalai Lama: The Good Heart

1995 Laurence Freeman: On Jesus

1996 Raimon Panikkar: The Silence of Life

1997 Mary McAleese: Reconciled Being

1998 Thomas Keating: The Heart of the World

1999 Huston Smith: Return to the Light

2000 The Dalai Lama and previous presenters:
      The Way of Peace

2001 Rowan Williams: Spirit in the Desert

2002 Kallistos Ware: Kingdom of the Heart—
      The Jesus Prayer in Daily Life

2003 Andrew Harvey, Shirley du Boulay, and
      Bruno Barnhart: Bede Griffiths

2004 Joan Chittister: Heart of Flesh—Feminist
      Spirituality for Men and Women

2005 Richard Rohr: A Lever and a Place to Stand